SERVE
INVESTING TOGETHER IN STUDENT MINISTRY

Serve: Investing Together In Student Ministry

Copyright © 2025 by Jody Dean. All rights reserved.
Published by youthministry360, in the United States of America.

ISBN 13: 9781954429611

No part of this publication may be reproduced, stored in a retrieval system, or trans- mitted in any form or by any means electronic or mechanical, including photocopy, audio recording, digital scanning, or any information storage and retrieval system now known or to be invented, without prior permission in writing from the publisher.

Any reference within this piece to Internet addresses of websites not under the administration of youthministry360 is not to be taken as an endorsement of these websites by youthministry360; neither does youthministry360 vouch for their content.

Unless otherwise noted, Scripture quotations are from the ESV® Bible (The Holy Bible, English Standard Version®), copyright © 2001 by Crossway, a publishing ministry of Good News Publishers. Used by permission. All rights reserved.

Managing Editor
Chris Hargrove

Director of Publishing
Kerry Ray

Art Director
Abby Hunt

SERVE
INVESTING TOGETHER IN STUDENT MINISTRY

BY JODY DEAN, PhD
FOREWORD BY DR. JAMIE DEW

PUBLISHED BY YM360

TABLE OF CONTENTS

Foreword..8

PART 1: WHY
Chapter 1: The Call to Serve......................................12
Chapter 2: Generational Impact................................17
Chapter 3: What is Teamwork..................................22
Chapter 4: Mentoring Disciple Servants...................27
Chapter 5: Personal Devotion (Giftedness and Fruitfulness)...34

PART 2: WHO
Chapter 6: C.A.R.E……………………………………………..42
Chapter 7: Self-Directed and Self-Motivated………………48
Chapter 8: Mindset of a Servant……………………………..55
Chapter 9: Engaged in the Local Church…………………..60
Chapter 10: Understanding of Youth Culture……………..66

PART 3: HOW
Chapter 11: Volunteers as a T.E.A.M.……………………….74
Chapter 12: Communication………………………………….80
Chapter 13: Navigating Issues and Challenges……………87
Chapter 14: Training and Equipping………………………..93
Chapter 15: Clarifying Questions…………………………….98

Conclusion……………………………………………………….104

Study Guide……………………………………………………..106

About the Author………………………………………………121

FOREWORD

As a former pastor who came to Christ after attending a youth camp as a young man, youth ministry has always had a special place in my heart. Although I am now the President of a seminary and have kids of my own who are the same age as I was when I came to Christ, I continue to recognize and appreciate the importance of youth ministry. Indeed, it is a calling that we simply cannot afford to overlook, nor can we overlook its significance for our denomination and the work we've been engaged in for generations. But even if we are sober-minded enough to appreciate the importance of this responsibility – the "why" of youth ministry – there still remains the crucial question of "how" to raise up leaders amongst our churches and how to equip them for effective gospel ministry to young men and women in our churches and around the world.

If you are a youth pastor or have ever worked in student ministry, you know that it can be messy. It takes more than slogans and life verses to navigate the ever-shifting terrain of youth ministry. It's volatile. It's rapidly changing at an ever-increasing rate. Ministering to students in a time like ours is certainly not for the faint of heart. But these same factors that make ministry difficult for pastors and youth leaders, are the very realities and dynamics younger generations face every day. Pluralism, nihilism, reactionary politics, libertinism, and relativism are, unfortunately, more than just professional obstacles to our ministry goals. They are the challenges that young men and women are inundated with in our culture every day and from every direction.

Now more than ever, it is incumbent upon us as a denomination of churches and as the body of Christ as a whole to focus our efforts for the sake of training up young generations unto truth and godliness – wielding the sword of truth but also the towel and basin of servanthood. Let us endeavor, with all sobriety and resoluteness, to take advantage of the harvest that has been set before us and get busy with the messy and beautiful work of raising up young disciples with which the Lord has stewarded us. That's why I am thankful for this book and the biblical principles it utilizes for effective strategies in developing biblically rooted and spiritually vibrant student ministries.

By identifying key principles for leadership in student ministry, like the importance of mentoring disciple servants, being engaged in one's local church, and facilitating teamwork among fellow laborers for the kingdom, this book walks through the ins and outs of student ministry. Whether considering the deeply personal and spiritual aspect of your call to ministry, the practical and strategic insights into how we can better be engaged in the culture of the youth we're called to serve, or even advice in navigating difficult issues and challenges unique to student ministry, this book can be a handbook and a resource for you to be a more effective leader.

Dr. Jamie Dew
President | New Orleans Baptist Theological Seminary

PART 1

WHY

In the following chapters, we tackle why we serve in student ministry. As we unpack the call for a Christian to serve, you may consider when you were called to follow Jesus and serve in the local church. The generational impact of investing in another generation and why we should be cultivated through serving as disciples will be addressed. Why should we serve as a team in student ministry? How do we continue to check our hearts on our personal devotion to ministry? We will unpack the compelling question of why we give of ourselves to the ministry of students.

CHAPTER 1
THE CALL TO SERVE

Serving on a team is something most people will do at some point in their life. A middle school group project, a leadership council in high school, a collegiate organization, or a staff team at work are some ways you may have experienced the joy or frustration of working with other people. In my experience, it's not uncommon to find out that leaders have experienced levels of frustration over collaborative work with others. In student ministry, we often hear about students' struggles on a sports team, group project, or student leadership organization at their school. You may have heard a student complaining about all the practice time without the coach putting them in the game or the student upset over doing all the work on a project while everyone earned the same grade. Learning to serve with others in a way that you do not care who gets the credit is an incredible snapshot into how John the Baptist prepared the way for Jesus (Matthew 3:3) or how the core group of twelve disciples around Jesus followed along the path of His ministry for months with a small piece of information being revealed in segments along their journey. Fast forward, and ministry volunteers struggle with solutions because a "Google" option has created a sense of an immediate answer to any question or problem. Over the years, I have loved to get large "Post-it" sheets or oversized dry-erase boards to brainstorm and problem-solve. My joy in solving a problem with markers and a blank space may cause anxiety for some people, but for me, it is invigorating.

You begin to mix various cultures, generations, and preferences with life experience, and we have a mixture of incredible skills and opportunities for ministry. Think of the disciples of Jesus day, and from them, He chose the group of twelve that we continue to read about. In your church, from the congregation, you select people to serve and be engaged in student ministry. You select from the student ministry those students who have demonstrated leadership potential. I am thankful each week for the men and women that came to mind from student ministry when I was a teenager. I had five unique student ministers in six years. I had over ten small group leaders who opened the Bible each week. I had numerous chaperones for retreats, camps, conferences, and mission trips. These countless ministers and volunteers do not include the ministry teams and leadership opportunities to serve others before graduating high school. The amazing aspect is that each student who begins and graduates high school has this level of investment from student ministry.

Each student has a youth minister, Bible teachers, chaperones, and opportunities to serve if they are willing and available. This testimony is why I believe understanding the "serve" capacity in your church and among your student ministry is an invaluable asset to cultivate for generational disciple impact for years to come. I can assure you I frustrated some ministers, volunteers, chaperones, and peers without a plan to do so. You may have a teenager on the verge of discovering salvation, the next step in their formation to be more like Christ, their call to ministry, or another aspect of the life of your church. This training involves collaboration and teamwork as disciples come together to serve. Equipping students, volunteers, chaperones, and Bible teachers is just one lens of executing the multiplication of people to understand and serve within the body of Christ with their gifts. They use their gifts and are trained or equipped to fit within a team, executing their giftedness and growing in their strengths and weaknesses. I have a study Bible that was given to me by one of my youth ministers, and it has several areas marked before it was given to me. Decades later, that means more to me now than it did the first time. I even studied some of the marked passages for the first time. Serve with a generational multiplication mindset. My youth minister had no idea I would one day teach those passages to hundreds of people in different churches and countries or a seminary classroom.

A simple call to serve is not glamorous. The towel and basin approach is messy, ugly, and yet beautiful all at the same time. The image of washing someone's smelly, sweaty, and ugly feet is not an appealing call to most people. Jesus, in a dusty dirt road culture, where sandals were the norm for footwear and where the custom was to wash your feet as you entered the home, modeled washing the disciple's feet. The image of a towel and basin as servants in student ministry creates a powerful mental picture for each of us that serves students and their families each week through the local church.

Jesus stated, "The harvest is plentiful, but the laborers are few" (Matthew 9:37). As we think about the Gospel, we understand that many still need to hear the good news of Jesus. We also can have a secondary interpretation that serving in ministry is also a challenge. More attend sitting in a row in worship than serve in a ministry throughout the week. Serving in student ministry is a great place for many adults to utilize their gifts in the local church. However, student ministry is not for every adult. We should invest in background checks and screening processes to shepherd minors from harm. The goal is to protect students from harm, whether from a peer or an adult. You may have picked up the book "Protect" to help you navigate structuring and executing your ministry around healthy shepherding guidelines with minors. I hope you continue to safeguard your work.

This book is intended for you to work through the content with those adults in your student ministry. Each area was prayed over and reviewed through the lens of student ministry—years of church staff and as a volunteer in student ministry were utilized. The lens of a parent of students was also factored into the writing. I spent time in the local church, trying to galvanize leaders, both students and adults, to give their time and resources to link arms and serve, which I discovered was a never-ending process. As a professor, I have been able to teach and train on these truths, as serving cultivation is an ongoing work and not an annual conference or event. When I am not serving in an interim capacity at a church, my time is invested in the student ministry at my local church. I get to chaperone camp, teach a small group of students, and help with various events, including our discipleship weekend with students. I share that not as a resume but for you as a reader to know this work is from a guy who has lived it and married an incredible woman who has faithfully served with me. The struggle to manage the needs of people in student ministry seems like half the battle some weeks. If the stomach bug is raging and your text messages are blowing up with people dropping out of teaching their small group for sickness, or you have planned an incredible event, and then a tournament gets changed due to weather and guts, many of your student leaders and volunteers from being able to attend and help, then depression of being a student minister can be challenging. Then, the other days come when just a regular youth worship service sparks a revival among students, and hope springs up that God is moving, lives are being changed, and that movement reveals the investment is worth it.

Ministry is never perfect or ideal, but God moments still happen. I have seen it countless times. For example, at camp, when God moved, it started with one student seen as a leader by some of their peers, who shared how

God was working in their lives. I was there when a senior adult man on a mission trip as a bus driver turned into a mentor of young high school guys. I was there when a faithful adult Bible study leader had a group catch fire for God's Word and began to invest beyond the allotted group meeting. I've seen girls keep bringing friends that eventually brought parents. These experiences and more are why we collectively invest and encourage people to serve and join the countless teams of generations that have been equipped for the work of ministry.

PAUSE & REFLECT

Who is someone who has modeled serving, and how has that impacted you?

Volunteering, leading, or team orientation may sound like the most boring time you will ever spend at church, but you all want to know what you're supposed to do and not look stupid, right? I mean, I might be asking for a friend. IYKYK.

A chaperone (curfew enforcer), teacher (expert Bible teacher that brings donuts), volunteer that monitors the crowd (hall monitor), head pizza slicer (stresses over whether there will be enough food), youth praise team member (cool hair guy that can play drums) wants to know what is expected of them. They need to know when to show up, where to be, why they were asked to be there, how they could prepare, and what is expected of them. These are some general expectations a random stranger may ask if you said, "Hey, would you like to serve?" A general understanding of the basics is a simple guideline for having a position description or general fact sheet for each aspect of student ministry to help people understand and commit to what is being asked of them through serving through a specific assignment.

QUESTIONS TO CONSIDER

1. Take a few minutes and write out your personal testimony and your call to serve within the church.

2. What is your capacity as a student ministry leader to nurture new volunteers?

3. Take a few moments to consider what it's like serving. Then, think about **WHY** you love serving in student ministry.

CHAPTER 2
GENERATIONAL IMPACT

Next-gen ministry is one of the greatest opportunities for intergenerational ministry in the local church. In any given week, this area of ministry has three to four generations interacting with one another. Student ministry will have three generations at a camp, retreat, or weekly gathering, allowing for diverse perspectives and life experiences. Student ministry can leverage generational influences to remind adults that the future is bright as students desire to grow in Christ and be a part of His Church. These adults who serve then share with other adults in the church to help the church understand the value of the younger generation and how students are needed. Senior adults are great with emerging adults by opening their homes to let college students serve together. Developing opportunities for intergenerational ministry is difficult at times, but the reward for the ministry makes an incredible impact on all the generations.

Some simple intergenerational student ministry ideas can be accomplished by having senior adult prayer partners for students when they go to camp, a young at heart Valentine's banquet for senior adults hosted by the student ministry, or senior adults making desserts for a youth retreat. Students can also serve younger kids by helping with music, recreation, or crafts during Vacation Bible School. Many churches utilize students paired with adults to serve on the praise team, in the media ministry, or on preschool rotations during worship. We can explain away many reasons why intergenerational relationships are complicated or challenging to navigate. Yes. Students can be fickle or not show up because they forgot or, at the last minute, decided to go to a friend's house for the weekend. A team-based approach to bringing people together to serve alongside one another and break down any barriers is a win for the Kingdom and the local church. Senior adults, adults, and emerging adults are needed beyond supporting camp or mission fundraisers through car washes or any other financial commitment to sending students elsewhere to serve and follow the Lord. Intergenerational ministry can be jump-started with a short-term mission trip with different generations teaching, serving, and growing together.

These are just small ways to begin to have an intergenerational impact from younger to older and older to younger within your church. This is not always easy and takes time, but the impact pays off immensely in the long term for student ministry and the church. A spotlight of an adult each week in your student ministry, a prayer time for older adults, or service mission days where you do chores for the elderly are simple ways to keep the generational impact of student ministry on the forefront without reshaping the entire student ministry. Being intentional in developing relationships with younger and older is all it takes to develop an intergenerational student ministry. For centuries, each generation has had to overcome its labels. You can take a cursory review of the last century and begin to see the differences between generations that emerged as well as ebbing and flowing as they matured. The student ministry of each church creates a glimpse of how the next generation will be received within the broader context of the local church.

As a youth leader, you must remind yourself to intentionally include various generations of adults in the student ministry.

PAUSE & REFLECT

Take a minute to review the people serving in your student ministry. Do you have a generation among your volunteers? How intergenerational is your student ministry?

Gentelligence can be a powerful connection for students. "Gentelligence champions every generation and is born from intergenerational curiosity. It's a willingness to understand how people who have grown up under different times view things differently and meaningfully. By viewing generational differences through a new lens, we can start to understand how they can be leveraged effectively."[1] Think about how many different generations are reflected in your student ministry through your church.

---

[1] Megan Gerhardt, Josephine Nachemson-Ekwall, and Brand Fogel, *Gentelligence: The Revolutionary Approach to Leading an Intergenerational Workforce* (New York, NY: Rowman & Littlefield, 2021),3.

Your students, their siblings, parents, grandparents, volunteers, and church members comprise many different generations. Review the current generations: Traditionalists born before 1945, Baby Boomers 1946-1964, Gen Xers 1965-1980, Millennials 1981-1998, Gen Z 1999-2019, and Alpha 2020 to the present.[2] As you think about them, you realize that there are six generations represented, five of whom are adults. This is the most generations living at one time and with a unique variance of life experience. This has not surprised God because He recorded the need for connection and communication across generations in His Word. Remember that in biblical times, it was common to have an extended family household with more than two generations living under the same roof.

> [4] "Hear, O Israel: The Lord our God, the Lord is one. [5] You shall love the Lord your God with all your heart and with all your soul and with all your might. [6] And these words that I command you today shall be on your heart. [7] You shall teach them diligently to your children, and shall talk of them when you sit in your house, and when you walk by the way, and when you lie down, and when you rise. [8] You shall bind them as a sign on your hand, and they shall be as frontlets between your eyes. [9] You shall write them on the doorposts of your house and on your gates."
> – Deuteronomy 6:4-9

Imagine someone born before World War II (1939) who may not have had electricity in their home or an automobile growing up. Today, you have current students who have technology that they have mastered. Think about all the various ways we can travel, access information, or the numerous opportunities available to people, as well as the need to understand one another and hear life stories and testimonies from adults across the lifespan. Senior adults can be prayer partners for the students during the school year. They can be paired with students to write notes of encouragement during camp. Parents need to be equipped to disciple their family; for most of them, this was not modeled for them as they were teenagers.

Generational differences can divide us if we allow them to cause division. Still, we can also find ways to create an intergenerational church and, more specifically, student ministry if we intentionally cultivate adults to serve. The landscape of gifts and talents in Scripture is needed in student

---

[2] Haydn Shaw, *Sticking Points: How to get 5 generations working together in the 12 places they come apart* (Carol Stream, IL: Tyndale Momentum, 2020), 10.

ministry. While some adults may be limited in their time or level of engagement, each person needs to be equipped and trained for what they are asked to do in any ministry. If students need a friend to spend time with, they have the resources to find that outside of the student ministry. Teenagers need adults who can be trusted mentors in their lives. A person that they can rely on to serve with integrity in all things. Adults must be recruited with a high standard of ministerial ethics to be sure those allowed to be around teenagers are people of the character who will not be prone to distract from the ministry but rather enhance the ongoing work with teenagers and their families.

Considerations with middle school begin with the fact that they were born in the last twelve to fifteen years. The adults around them today remember the first-generation iPhone and may have owned an iPod before that. A majority of adults can remember their life without social media. Middle school students can benefit from the influence of multiple generations of adults investing in their spiritual formation. This can help them with their worldview, navigating culture, developing their theological framework, and understanding their involvement in the church, which are just a few ways a gentelligent focus can impact their development.

High school students are moving closer to adulthood at an earlier age. They are beginning to have their first job, they want more individual freedom with peers and driving, some begin to date, and they actually desire more and more to be adults. They may not desire all the adult responsibilities that being an adult brings, but they desire the idea of adulthood. A gentelligent focus can help them understand and learn from the struggles of various generations and how they would have made different life choices.

QUESTIONS TO CONSIDER

1. Describe some ways you think the student ministry could become more intergenerational.

2. Why is it important to approach ministry with an intergenerational mindset?

3. How can you become more gentelligent with various generations as you work together?

CHAPTER 3
WHAT IS TEAMWORK?

Team has different connotations for the different generations found inside a local church. Each age group has different experiences with the concept of a team, whether a sports team or a group project. In a local church, when people begin to serve, they become part of a greater web of relationships of people who work together to accomplish a host of ministries each week. Teenagers of the last several generations have had leadership fail them. The biggest need outside of salvation through faith alone in Christ alone is to be in a local church community where relationships are nurtured and opportunities to serve are available. A mentor who is willing to disciple a person as part of a team for serving in ministry is a great way to help someone on their journey. Each servant is on a personal journey to become more like Christ, and as a student ministry leader, you can help cultivate others along the way. Ponder some of the stories in the Bible, like Jethro speaking into Moses, Eli and Samuel, Elizabeth and Mary, or Paul into Timothy, where an adult mentored another disciple. They each mentored someone toward Christlikeness.

As you commit to serving, you are now in the league of heroes who help the local church pull off incredible work during one of our most awkward and vulnerable times. If you look at the middle school picture of yourself, you probably hope your grandma does not display that memory forever.

The *awkwardness* of middle school fades and ushers in the *attitude* of high school in all its glory. These two "a's" occur so that we can obtain adulthood later. It seems that in high school, the approach taken is to prove oneself, defend one's position, reveal one's feelings toward the issues of life, and one's feelings toward authority, to name a few. Adolescence has now extended into the college years as the markers of previous generations for being an adult have been delayed. Society has moved the goalposts again for adulthood. We also have more generations coexisting than ever before. The great aspect is that each adult generation can contribute by serving in student ministry.

Does everyone put in the same amount of time and effort on the team? Do I receive fair recognition? People naturally have personal and maybe selfish questions on a team. Some weeks, it feels like we may be more invested than others in the work on the team. If you pivot to thinking that the work is a collective kingdom effort, then the individual is not the focus. Still, the overall ministry being accomplished as an overall team that you as a person are a vital part of each week should be the focus of the ministry team. People coming together to accomplish the ministry collectively is the ideal, but functionally, how does that quantify into a working model in your ministry setting?

Questions range for some team members about effort and recognition, but being a part of the team is simply doing your part and not judging others for their part in the work. We may not know all that another team member is doing with counseling a student, praying, and serving through other visible ways, which are good reminders that the big picture of teamwork is to pull our weight on the team. As servants called to be a part of the body of Christ, we utilize our gifts and talents on our team in a way that pulls our own weight. Being a faithful team member does not mean you are entitled or responsible to voice how you think others should be serving. The overall concept is that together, a team can do more than an individual serving alone. As you link arms with others in ministry, more people will be excited and willing to engage in the work. Utilize your influence to encourage more students and adults to participate as team members. You can show others what it means to serve and how to be a good team member.

PAUSE & REFLECT

Consider the following verses from Ephesians 4:11-16 to be reminded about the different gifts that make up the body and how we come together to do ministry as a team (one body).

[11] And he gave the apostles, the prophets, the evangelists, the shepherds and teachers, [12] to equip the saints for the work of ministry, for building up the body of Christ, [13] until we all attain to the unity of the faith and of the knowledge of the Son of God, to mature manhood, to the measure of

the stature of the fullness of Christ, [14] so that we may no longer be children, tossed to and fro by the waves and carried about by every wind of doctrine, by human cunning, by craftiness in deceitful schemes. [15] Rather, speaking the truth in love, we are to grow up in every way into him who is the head, into Christ, [16] from whom the whole body, joined and held together by every joint with which it is equipped, when each part is working properly, makes the body grow so that it builds itself up in love.

TEAMWORK WITH MIDDLE SCHOOLERS
Middle schoolers have the insight of a sports team or a group project in their schoolwork. Collaboration to accomplish a goal or objective is common among the younger generations when developing their interpersonal skills. In their younger years, parents help to schedule their lives so that they can have social interaction. In middle school, their team involvement at school, church, and extracurricular options become more personal choices. In student ministry, you can find ways to help them cultivate their understanding of being a healthy team member and how to nurture a thriving team.

TEAMWORK WITH HIGH SCHOOLERS
High schoolers have team experiences, which can include their first work environment. As a student ministry, you can come alongside students to equip them to be effective in their youth group and in their team environments of school, work, and extracurricular activities. The desire to be a leader and a valued team member can develop a student's lifetime healthy understanding of being a value-added team member—a person who adds value to the environments where they get to serve and lead.

TEAMWORK WITH COLLEGE STUDENTS
College students thrive in being on intramural sports teams and organizations for student leadership. Many have jobs and work in collaborative environments for their career plans. Emerging adults are vital to being equipped for teamwork for the rest of their lives. In these formative years, from middle school through emerging adulthood, the development aspects of life are the prime years where a person is disciplined to be a team leader and team member who walks with Christ. The collegiate ministry opportunities rely on student leadership to accomplish their ministry. College students can also be an asset in many church ministry areas, including student ministry. As a college freshman, the first year after high school can be tricky as life transitions are often challenging.

TEAMWORK WITH ADULTS

Adults have life experiences that influence their perceptions of teamwork and what it means to be a team member. It is important to know how people perceive being on a team and what participation they have had on teams. In the team member vetting process, it is always good to ask people about their previous experiences being a part of a team as well as their experiences serving in church. Adults have a lot of life experience that can make being a good team member a challenge. If they are used to being the leader at work, then being a simple participatory member of a serving team may take more coaching. Sometimes, adults need to know the type of team meetings and input that will be expected. Some meetings are informal and fellowship-oriented to develop relationships among team members. Formal meetings are needed at times to provide important information. Collaborative meetings are needed when overall input from team members is needed for planning or developing ministry details for weekly ministry programming.

Teamwork cultivation is an integral part of the ministry that was modeled in how Jesus equipped the twelve disciples who chose to follow His leadership. A group of diverse people with different life and work experiences of various ages begin their journey of learning to work together and do life together while following Jesus on His earthly ministry rhythm. We will not have a team for the exact same reasons that Jesus cultivated this ragamuffin group of guys, but we will have people who desire to come alongside the work and help carry it on into the future. In our ministries, we will probably not be asked to leave our home and daily rhythm for the most part, as these guys did. The simple task of fulfilling the mission of being a part of a team is to be found faithful in your work and committed to the overall health of the ministry.

QUESTIONS TO CONSIDER

1. What has been your favorite team to be a member of? Why?

2. If you were creating a team member requirement list of expectations, what would they be? Explain your expectations to fellow team members or leaders when you can.

3. How do you see yourself as a team member? A supportive advocate, a questioning participant, a loyal member who is eager to help, or a hesitant to speak up but faithful team member. You may not be one of these, but put your thoughts in your own words.

Being a healthy team member takes work and is an ongoing process. As you serve in your student ministry, it is crucial to be a devoted disciple who is faithful to your church. In the next chapter, we will focus on your growth as a disciple.

CHAPTER 4
MENTORING DISCIPLE SERVANTS

Developing disciples into growing believers is not an easy task, and when you add the changes and pressures from different stages of development, then you have a mixture of challenges and considerations for discipleship. Generation Z is the generation that is growing up during a challenging time navigating technology and relationships. One research study provided insight into the fact that students raised within a religious environment are happier and healthier. In addition, those students with religious upbringing and community have psychological and behavioral benefits that they carry beyond childhood into adulthood.[3] Mentoring is the term I gravitate toward for investing in people so that they can grow into the disciple servants Christ is calling each of us to become.

A mentor can mean something different to each person, but in Scripture, I am drawn to Paul and Timothy. A more mature believer in Paul chooses Timothy to invest his life and ministry to the extent both are impacted for Christ. Considerations for their relationship can be examined, with only a mother and grandmother listed for Timothy in Scripture and the importance of a male Christian for Timothy, as Paul listed in his second letter to Timothy (2 Timothy:1:1-6). Plans had to be a part of the relationship regarding travel, provision, and integrity. They had to navigate the culture, family, and ministry as they worked together in an effort to minister to the churches. Issues and struggles arose, as we can see in the letters Paul wrote to Timothy and the churches. As we begin to think

---

[3] https://ifstudies.org/blog/religious-upbringing-and-adolescence

about mentoring and developing disciples in student ministry, we will look at four different age groups: middle schoolers, high schoolers, emerging adults in college, and adults as parents of students. We will examine in light of Paul and Timothy's considerations, plans, areas to navigate, and issues to overcome as we mentor disciples in student ministry.

MENTORING MIDDLE SCHOOLERS

Mentoring middle school students is different because of how boys and girls develop in this age group. Amy Byrd provides great insight into girl's ministry. "Think about all that your girls experience from the time you get them in middle school to the day that they walk across the stage at graduation. They will work and fight through several issues — body image, purity, friendships, dating relationships, identity in Christ, and modesty. This list is just the tip of the iceberg when it comes to the life of a teenage girl and all that she will walk through in her time as a student."[4]

Age differences can shape the approach we take to mentoring students, and the most obvious we have during the adolescent years can be explained through the lens of the four age gaps. I have a saved article on my computer from Shane Pruitt that has reminded me of the four age gaps in student ministry. The first age gap is between middle school and high school.[5] Think of the middle school boy whose mother asks him to take out the trash. An hour later, she comes through the kitchen and says, "Son, what about the trash?" He responds, "Oh yeah, I forgot," and then he takes out the trash.

Now imagine saying to that same guy to memorize Scripture, read his Bible, or share his faith with a friend, and you are reminded of the ongoing need to remind and teach middle school guys the truth over and over. Hence, it begins to become more profound as they mature toward high school.

A middle school girl has some similar concerns to a guy but is different from the ongoing emotion of mean girls, likes, and social media influences for body image. Guys have some of these distractions, but girls are navigating being comfortable with themselves as well as being comfortable with others. The bottled emotion is an ongoing struggle through the upperclassman years in high school. The father begins to realize his baby girl is maturing, and her relationship with her parents changes. The mentor can speak truth into her life in ongoing ways,

---

[4] https://studentministry.lifeway.com/2014/08/19/how-to-minister-to-girls-in-your-student-ministry/
[5] https://www.gensend.org/resource/first-person-addressing-the-four-major-gaps-in-student-ministry/

showing that she is beautiful and created in God's image. The truths of God and spiritual practices must be reinforced each week for guys and girls.

If your group is large enough, this age can benefit from small groups and mentorship by gender so they can deal with and discuss (if they are willing to ever open up) their struggles.

PAUSE & REFLECT

Discuss ways to speak the truth and mentor middle school students in your ministry. What are some safeguards with minors you need to consider with age-gender-specific mentoring opportunities?

MENTORING HIGH SCHOOLERS

The mentoring of high schoolers begins to take a different shape from middle school as they have more flexibility, begin to drive, and are available for times outside the typical church schedule. This highlights another age gap, which is the driver's license gap among high school students. However, that also means their time is pulled between work, school, church, and their increasing social calendars. You will find differences with your high school students as your students experience all the final moments of their senior year of high school while preparing for college or their vocation.

The journey for students, parents, and leaders as they walk through the senior year ups and downs is one of those separating factors for students to move more toward feeling like adults. The struggles in school of navigating life only get more complicated as the high schooler has to begin to figure out how to launch into adulthood. They have to consider a career or at least a college major or trade program. The gap year model has become popular to take a year between high school and college to help figure out life and what you desire to do in life while traveling the world, serving on mission, or an internship program that offers some college credit for the one-year commitment.

One aspect of mentoring students should include helping them navigate high school milestones. As we mentor students to live the Christian life, they are also trying to survive high school, so they need help with everyday challenges. Guys and girls have differences that mirror the challenges of middle school but at a more mature level. Body image, academics, and learning to navigate communication differences are all examples that high school students are experiencing each week. These challenges continue from high school into the college years.

MENTORING COLLEGE STUDENTS
This may be the sweetest season for mentoring for the 18–25-year-olds in your ministry. An emerging adult age can be fondly referred to by adults for the rest of their lives. College is where many adults meet the love of their life, learn independence, and discover a strong community of friends. Everything begins to click together for the emerging adult. As mentors, you begin to have deeper conversations over Scripture and how to live the Christian life. Your mentor may be an upper classmate who is just a few years ahead of you but can help you navigate all the gaps from high school to college. The movement between high school and college brings learning curves with more than roommates, course schedules, and where to travel on your winter break.

College students can be great mentors for high school students in helping them, but they may still need a mentor. The college years are fond memories for many from their campus ministry involvement and how their faith was nurtured in college through their friends and opportunities to serve their church and their campus. Both campus ministries that I got to be a part of their leadership were trying but very rewarding. I took students on their first mission trip out of the country, nurtured many worldview questions, and answered many questions about other religions as students encountered various belief systems with classmates. Many churches have college students and need to help mentor them to live through the challenge of feeling connected at school but maybe disconnected at church since they are no longer in student ministry. A college campus has energy and constant activity like our student ministries do in the church, but the collegiate ministry at church feels different from their student ministry experience of high school.

Another consideration for college students is the fact that many discover their faith in college and need a mentor for their new walk with the Lord. You have the spectrum of devoted students to new believers together, but in college, the group size has shrunk. A youth group is a larger group of students, but many college groups in churches are smaller in size and thus have a different vibe for the student to adjust to at church. A college student has limited experience as a mentor and may struggle to help their peers develop their new faith.

MENTORING ADULTS
As an adult or parent, you have the great opportunity to come alongside college students and build a relationship to mentor them. Consider asking:

Are you a person worthy of being followed? Paul writes about being an example in several of his letters. Look at what he said in his letter to Philippi: "Brothers join in imitating me, and keep your eyes on those who walk according to the example you have in us." (Philippians 3:17)

Developing other people to grow in their relationship and serve in ministry through the church is a natural path for the Christian. This natural rhythm of investing your life into others is not a new concept because we see examples modeled for us in Scripture. Although you may respond to the thought well, of course, Jesus did, but you have many other examples. Barnabas and Paul modeled investing into partners in ministry to the extent it caused them to part ways and multiply their ministry as we read Acts 15. The use of Paul's word, entrust, in 2 Timothy 2:2 is a word that reminds us of passing on something that lasts to another generation.

As Christians, we are called to ministry and have a purpose of service in our churches. Cultivating people to recognize they are ministers as disciples and should have a ministry is why pastors continue to ask for people to serve. The student ministry is one of those areas of service in the church that many have invested in having a pastor, minister, or director on the staff. Many churches rely on a volunteer coordinator because the cost is too much for the church budget to pay a staff member. Some people suggest that each person serving in ministry should consider who they should invest in to replace them; however, we never do that to retire from ministry. The concept is intended to multiply to another generation of disciple leaders.

Many people do not consider the generous posture of giving their time through serving the church as a leader, servant, teacher, or minister. One of the generous aspects of giving of our life in Christ is giving our time to someone or something else. The Church is the best place to be generous with our wealth and time. An apprentice is the term utilized for the understudy for a vocation. A mentee for someone on their spiritual journey of being poured into by a more mature Christ follower. Can you begin to imagine the countless hours spent each week by volunteers serving on various teams in churches around the world? The millions upon millions of hours per week. If the world had only 500,000 churches and an average of 50 volunteer hours per week per church, we would reach 25 million volunteer hours per week. Developing others to join the effort to be generous through their time by serving and developing others is a needed task for student ministry. If you are reading this book, chances are you have leadership responsibility within your church's student ministry, and you probably could use a few more volunteer hours if someone is willing to be generous and join your team.

People miss church due to sickness, vacation, work, and other reasons with family, and as a result, you always need to mind the gaps each week. Every ministry is different, but most of us would probably agree that a 25% cushion on the team is often necessary to mind the gap for those who are unavailable any given week. Some weeks, I would have twenty-five adults to serve for the mid-week worship and discipleship time, and other weeks, everyone's life aligned to where I might not have five or ten. A simple aspect of developing others is to have a list of those being cultivated as potential team members. A potential Bible study leader, chaperone, or student ministry volunteer may need time to be vetted, but they also need to be comfortable with the responsibility. Sometimes, joining the team can feel more like a service from a posture of guilt or obligation and not generosity.

1. Ponder and make a list of possible team members to be vetted.

2. Now, take that list and pray for each person.

3. How many of those names do you know of their personal testimony or ministry story?

4. Take out your phone and text to see if you can have coffee or a meal to learn their story.

Make it a point to do this every few weeks throughout the year or monthly at a minimum. Even if you know the people's stories, it is good to be refreshed in your knowledge. Be sure when you meet with people to find out any updates and ask what the Lord is teaching them through His Word and His Church.

This is just one simple way to develop others to serve within your weekly rhythm. An encouraging word or refreshing time with another believer or a few can be life-giving for each of you involved. Often, those serving with students have less adult interaction during their time at church, so this can help them develop meaningful connections with other team members. I also would like to remind you that meetings alone should have accountability and parameters at all costs.

QUESTIONS TO CONSIDER

1. How generous do you consider yourself to be with your time?

2. How generous are you with others?

3. Could you be labeled as someone with favorites in your family, work, or church? If yes, then why?

CHAPTER 5
PERSONAL DEVOTION (GIFTEDNESS & FRUITFULNESS)

Devotion is a word used to describe the commitment between a married couple. The word can be used to frame a student's commitment to a sport, art, or academic pursuit. The term can describe our personal devotion to following the Lord. In this chapter, we will look at the term from the lens of devotion to the local church.

A lens for how we frame our discussion about devotion will be one that can be debated. A generation or two ago, church devotion differed from today, as people were committed to the church schedule and program. Those of us who have been in ministry for a few decades or involved in the local church for a longer season of time understand the shift from people spending devoted time on Sunday morning and evening as well as a mid-week evening to the local church and the ministries of that church. Many had youth events on the weekends, and student ministry extended that devotion to being a weekly commitment of an easy ten hours when you factor in volunteer hours, worship, Bible study, and events. The list is not exhaustive, but it gives you the idea of a clip art calendar that is full of activity and time together. Thank you for humoring a walk down the student ministry memory lane. Still, the context is needed to understand how we need to leverage our available moments with students today. The devotion of days gone by involved people being committed to a schedule and the programs of student ministry in the church, just like with the music, small group, or children's ministry areas of the church. The area you served became your tribe, and you worked together, encouraged one another, and developed relationships.

Today, we still tend to navigate toward a tribe. We see this in travel ball, scouts, gymnastics, fitness, and school. People have more places to develop a community around their activity to the degree that the church is not the primary driver for community for all the people that attend. This is why I believe that as we develop a culture of serving in our ministry, we must develop people who understand the need to be a tribe that can run together and help one another. Think about a tribe with diverse spiritual gifts, talents, and interests. Imagine that group of adults having a shared passion to reach the student generation of the season. Many in this tribe have discipled multiple seasons of students as they move through adolescence. Sometimes, we love this tribe to the point that we do not consider how we best fit into the ministry picture. In Scripture, Paul writes about the imagery of a body and how the different pieces fit together in our skeletal system (1 Corinthians 12).

I'd encourage you to take a spiritual gift test if you have never done one before. With a quick online search, you can find plenty of free options. A spiritual gift test is not intended to be conclusive but informative so that you can understand your natural indications toward areas of gifting. You will be more devoted when serving in areas that are natural for you to live out how the Lord created you. A diversity of gifts is needed in your church. In student ministry, you have a range of understanding of personal giftedness. The middle school guy who feels awkward in his changing body will embrace gifting differently from the parent serving faithfully as a volunteer.

In Ephesians 4:1-16, Paul speaks about the body functioning together as a body. This illustration of the people coming together within the local community of believers has application to a team of student ministry leaders and students using their gifts to serve. Consider all the different ways middle school, high school, college, and adults can serve together. Leading worship, teaching, administrating events and processes, retreats, outreach, fellowship, and building community are just some ways the student ministry can work together, utilizing their giftedness. I consider my spiritual gifts, which are the strongest on an inventory, to be the easiest to rely on in serving others instead of those that score less on the gift indicator. They are natural and come to the forefront before anything else. Although the list of gifts includes giving and mercy that may not be as strong as teaching or administration for me, I still need to have a personal devotion to have a composite in my journey with Christ to give and be merciful. Consider your own profile for gifts; in your composite snapshot of gifts, what would be easier or more natural for you? Do you have some areas that are a real struggle for you to serve? Natural gifting is needed in the body, and when we come together, we complete an image of who Christ intended the church to reflect. As we grow in our relationship with Christ and become stronger in our devotion to Christ and His Church, then we can have a different snapshot. Self-awareness in how we serve and our natural indicators of devotion serve as gauges for you as you serve and for the health of the ministry team.

Each student minister should have a process for nurturing spiritual gifts that they believe is the best fit for their church. The challenge is to employ that process so that each person within the ministry, student and adult, can be developed to serve within the local church utilizing their gifts. The most extraordinary growth for Christians comes through their personal devotion to the Lord and linking arms out of their dedication to serve others and their church. Many students and adults serve in other ministries of the church as well as within student ministry. When you consider serving and devotion, it is wise to look at the bigger picture of your church and not just the student ministry where students and adults are serving.

PAUSE & REFLECT

Now consider your devotion and contemplate and meditate on how you are doing. What can you tweak to leverage more devotion toward Christ, others, and His Church? This question is one that we should ask ourselves consistently.

A personal devotion indicator scale or a devotion inventory would not indicate the level of devotion that you have, but assessments, scales, or inventories that do exist can help you discern ways to invest your life through personal devotion to Christ and His Church. I have taken many leadership and discipleship-focused assessments that are not 100 percent accurate, but most of the time, they reflect my life and ministry tendencies. I am an extrovert who enjoys being around people who find the details life-giving. A guy who is gifted with teaching and exhorting but has the gift of administration. You might be surprised if you don't know me. My mercy level is low on most assessments, but Christ still calls me to be merciful. The indicators show me the areas that are life-giving and natural for me, but they do not give me a free pass for giving, mercy, compassion, or meekness. Traits, talents, and gifts are dispersed among the body of Christ, so when we gather, we make a complete team to devote ourselves to the work. Now, you can find several of these assessments for free online or pay a few dollars to take different ones.

In his writing, Luke revealed a lifestyle of devotion found among the early church in Acts 2. They were devoted to Christ and one another. They naturally gave of their time faithfully each week and most days, not one-time events per week. As you read, it is intriguing how they fellowshipped, prayed, and taught the Word to one another. These are collective aspects of devotion because Acts 2:42 states, "They devoted themselves." Apostles taught how to follow the Lord and develop personal devotion and fellowship through eating together and praying. Devotion for us should have the teaching, fellowship, and prayer components within the student ministry team. The results are also inspiring because they were filled with awe. Also, signs and wonders were being performed, and they were together and found all things in common. They were committed (devoted) to one another to the extent that they shared their resources.

We see an interesting snapshot of devotion from the early church. They modeled a clear devotion to Christ and His Church, a devotion to one another, and a devotion to corporate praise and worship. This passage has been studied and dissected over the centuries, but I want you to read Acts 2:42-47 and highlight all the aspects of devotion in any of these three areas that you see.

A coach will ask more of us during a game or season, and as an example of spirited competition, Paul shares of giving it all in the race. This example should serve to remind us to train and give in personal devotion as a runner competing for a prize. Devotion through service will be more assertive at times for people, and we should be able to cheer one another on and keep striving for our devotion to the Lord.

QUESTIONS TO CONSIDER

1. What did you learn about yourself from taking a spiritual gifts test?

2. Share about gifts that are not as strong and encourage ways to enhance those areas while serving through your strengths.

3. What practices help you each week with your devotion to serving Christ and His Church?

PART 2

WHO

Now that we have discussed why we should serve in student ministry, our attention will pivot to who should serve in student ministry. The people are the greatest asset to the student ministry, and several aspects of who serves are important to ponder as you serve on the team. The first consideration is the motives of those who serve and the care they take in their ministry. Another consideration is the self-directed ability of the servant, and the motivation that drives their service is essential as we consider who serves in student ministry. As you consider who serves in student ministry, the mindset that those serving are servants is an important consideration. The servant should be engaged in the local church and not just in the student ministry, which is an important consideration when allowing a person to serve in youth ministry. The final aspect in considering people to serve in the youth ministry is their understanding of the culture that students are navigating, as well as the culture being cultivated for students and their families to grow in their relationship with Christ and His Church.

CHAPTER 6
C.A.R.E.

The right people with the right motives are needed in student ministry. A simple acronym of C.A.R.E has guided me for several decades of student ministry. I desire to see people who are committed to Christ and His Church. I desire to see people who are available consistently to the students and the work so that trust can be built with students. I desire to see people who are relatable in their communication to the appropriate age of maturity of the students. I desire to see people who are examples that are reliable for students to replicate in their own lives. I believe this shepherding principle of C.A.R.E is simple but translates our desire to see adults serve that exhibit a genuine "care" focus through their service.

COMMITTED

How do you define commitment? You may have a memory of a guy being accused of having commitment issues in dating—the drama surrounding the conflict among the dating couple and the different lenses through which this is viewed. The level of commitment in a dating couple in high school can be awkward for many people in the student ministry and how the climate of the relationship impacts others. We see this even more within a marriage. A commitment to one another for better or worse, in sickness and in health, until death, is a high level of being sure you are in a relationship. Marriage is the image Christ uses to describe His relationship with the Church (Ephesians 5). As we think about the universal Church in this imagery of the Church as Christ's bride, let's keep that image in our minds as we explore individual commitment to serving the Church, specifically student ministry. I want you to picture the ideal wedding. This could be a wedding you attended, one you dream of, or your actual wedding. What made it so special? The couple, the setting, the people, the cake, or the dancing? What do you think makes us as the Church so special to Christ as you consider the relationship Christ has with you and His Church?

Now, with this mindset, ponder the characteristics of being a committed follower and servant in your church. Commitment can be something we struggle with as students and adults. As we age and mature, the challenges of living life in relationships with others are complicated. We struggle in our relationship with Christ, and in similar ways, we struggle in our commitment to others. Commitment issues are not our focus for the chapter, but being a committed team member in student ministry will be the lens we unpack. We first need to ponder our commitment.

Students desire to have people that will show up for them. This requires commitment from volunteers to get to know students and develop relationships with them and their families.

Available
Volunteers should be available to serve. People will naturally have conflicts and times of being unavailable, but a volunteer who is consistently unavailable or backing out of serving in their assigned capacity creates double work for the ministry leadership. 24/7 availability is a struggle for any staff member or volunteer in the rhythm of life. The concept is that you are faithful to be a part of a team that is consistently present. You are willing to be a person who only sometimes has a conflict or has a schedule that takes you away from serving more than you are available to be present.

Do you ever find yourself in a setting with people who are not present to participate, engage with others, or even worship? Let's be honest with one another; we all have moments when we are not fully present. This can happen when we serve students, worship with our church family, or even with our family at home. We have many distractions that prevent us from being present with others, one of those being a smartphone. Maybe you do not struggle with being present, but you feel pulled in many directions at church. You have gifts that can be utilized in several areas of the church and struggle to be fully available to all the areas you have said yes to serve. You may need to take a moment and consider all the things you have made yourself available for and determine if you have over-committed your availability.

Relatable
You do not have to buy a new wardrobe or learn a new vocabulary, but you must naturally relate to teenagers to connect with them. You have observed the grandparent who naturally gels with their teenage grandchildren and those who don't know how to carry on a conversation. This is true for adults of any age because sometimes the generation just

a little older can have the most challenging time connecting because they think they know how when they may struggle with being unrelatable. You may not naturally relate to students as you serve, but you can grow in this area and develop opportunities to connect with students.

Sometimes, the age gap allows an older adult to speak a new truth into the life of a younger student. I have seen older adults school some guys on Ping Pong, and the students are just amazed that the old guy has skills they never knew he had. Girls have connected around learning the skill of knitting or baking with an older lady. We have more natural ways to be relatable by just being open to sharing the wisdom we have gained already in this life. Adults of all ages have many aspects of their journey that can be relatable to students.

EXAMPLE

At the end of the day, I needed adults that could be an example that could be followed. Each generation of student ministry relies on adults that can be replicated through their lives into another generation. You may be aware of the team member who shows up to teach and has not prepared and plans just to wing it. This is not the example students need. The chaperone is begrudgingly off work and not happy to be there but does not want their student to go on the trip without them. The staff member who seems to always desire to be elsewhere or wants you to know what a sacrifice of time it is to be present can be a drain on the whole team.

The example of the teacher who prepares in such a way that you are always encouraged to want to be a teacher like that or to be the fun chaperone that people gravitate toward because their charismatic desire to be present is captivating. The staff member leads from a posture that student ministry is life-giving for them and that students are a priority in their lives. These are examples of what we aspire for in student ministry. Yes, bad days happen, and we can always have moments where we feel inadequate or feel divided between commitments with work and family.

C.A.R.E. provides a holistic snapshot of being the right type of leader in student ministry who is committed, available, and relatable. It is also an example that can motivate students to aspire to be this type of Christian in the local church.

PAUSE & REFLECT

The big takeaway for you is to first reflect on how you are doing with C.A.R.E. as a person. Does your service have a genuine focus that exhibits C.A.R.E.?

C.A.R.E. WITH MIDDLE SCHOOLERS
A middle school student can be committed, available, relatable with others, and an example for others. Think about a middle school student who is committed to their walk with the Lord, the youth group, and their church. Many students come to mind at my church when I think of these qualities and see middle school students who are faithful and express Christlikeness. Students who are available by being willing to serve and jump into serving within the youth ministry. During a retreat, at camp, or just at a large group gathering, you observe a middle school student reaching out to a student who is sitting by themselves or not just naturally grafting into the group and is available to minister to the student. You see many examples of a student that is reliable by following through with their commitments. If they sign up to help, then they show up and are ready to serve. This type of middle school student is an example that other students naturally are drawn to and desire to emulate.

C.A.R.E. WITH HIGH SCHOOLERS
Much like a middle school student, a high school student can be committed, available, relatable, and an example for others. Several students probably come to mind as you consider the students you know that model C.A.R.E. in their lives. As students gain more flexibility, some high schoolers choose to be more committed than their parents or other adults. The commitment of students can be remarkable as they have many options that ask them to be available, and they choose the student ministry. As they mature, you see a desire to be relatable to other students. Older students making themselves available to disciple other students is refreshing to observe as a youth leader. The older high school students becoming an example that other students and adults are inspired to nurture and follow can breathe life into the overall student ministry in ways adults do not have the same influence to cultivate. When the Lord moves the high school students to care, then it catches within the ministry in a natural multiplying effect.

C.A.R.E. WITH EMERGING ADULTS
Social causes, mission opportunities, and volunteer service register with college students that inspire them to be committed, available, relatable, and to be an example for others. Emerging adults can serve as leaders

and mentors for teenagers as they show maturity in Christ, a commitment to their church, and a model for staying available through their church as they move into adulthood. The relatability of emerging adults with students is in ways other leaders may struggle to connect in the same way as an example for students. The vetting process should be involved to ensure that emerging adults are modeling their private lives in the same ways observed within the church.

C.A.R.E. WITH ADULTS

Adults' life experiences give them perspective on what commitment means to the organization, as well as their personal impressions of being on a team and the varying levels of team members' commitment. Availability varies among adults based upon their life stage, such as marriage, kids, empty nest, or aging parents. Adults may have additional commitments that impact their availability with their work or family. The relatability with students can vary among adults as they may relate better among the volunteers and staff than with students, but the opposite can also be true. You have probably worked with an adult who could relate to students better than peers. Adults who walk with the Lord and model the level of care that is desired become the best examples of mentors for fellow team members and students.

QUESTIONS TO CONSIDER

1. What can you tweak in your schedule to have greater availability? If you are doing all that you can, then pray for those around you and yourself to stay focused and available to the youth ministry.

2. Relatability is a piece that can change for us as our stage in life changes or other priorities emerge. How are you relating with others on the team? Who is someone you relate to the most? Why?

3. Living life as an example for others to follow is a high calling. Paul instructed us to live as others can see the Christian life through our everyday walk with the Lord. How are you doing? How are you caring for the students and their families around you? Maybe you even need to ask how you are caring for yourself and your family.

CHAPTER 7
SELF-DIRECTED AND SELF-MOTIVATED

Do you consider yourself to be a self-starter? A person who can be given an idea and just run with it is your favorite assignment as a team member. You are able to find motivation each week to accomplish your responsibilities in ministry without being a procrastinator. I joke with students all the time that we have a procrastinator support group, but unfortunately, they have not met because they keep postponing their meetings.

SELF-MOTIVATED LEADER
A self-motivated leader has an internal drive to accomplish their goals and tasks and can complete those with little external motivation to accomplish their work. Motivation can be found throughout your week as you think about your focus, desires, temptations, challenges, and goals. You can be motivated to work out or lose weight for your health. You can have pure motivation that is not directed toward good things, as we are self-directed in how we determine how we spend our time and who we entrust with our friendship or affection. You see these aspects among students as well as adults in the church. The lunch line or the student section in a school can reveal a lot about how we are motivated. Some students never eat in the cafeteria and choose to bring their lunch and find a place with a few friends to isolate. Adults should model a walk with the Lord that displays fruit from their relationship with Christ. We have a motivation to live for Christ. I am motivated to study to teach my students entrusted to me each week so that they can hear, understand, and apply God's Word. This motivation is because of the accountability to teach well as the Lord requires more of a teacher but also to be a good teacher for the students.

SELF-DIRECTED LEADER
A self-directed leader is one who understands the mission and can execute each week with little coaching. They follow the outline of what is expected but can carry on without a leader being hands-on, reminding them how to do the work. Self-directed people are the true north for leaders in student ministry. A chaperone at camp who sees a struggling camper and is motivated to sit with them and coach them or listen to their story model's student ministry self-motivation. The mom who coordinates the food and set-up for an event or the dad who is willing to drive the van or bus for events are self-motivated volunteers who are needed. A student leader who is always compelled to seek out the students who are alone and without community and bring them into the group to be better connected is a great self-directed student leader. Different personalities can display other characteristics of being a self-directed team member. I have always enjoyed those who will just jump in and help get the task completed or the students engaged in what we are doing.

SERVANT LEADER
A servant leader is one who sees something needs to be done and is one who does not wait for instructions for simple needs. If trash needs to be picked up or someone needs encouragement, the servant team member is willing to simply serve as needs arise. You see this during events like camp, where the team needs people who look for ways to help and do not simply wait on the sidelines for someone to tell them to serve. Think about being a servant. Now, think about being a servant who is self-directed in the work. You know the mission and are ready to do your part without having to be begged. Now, think about being a servant who is self-directed and motivated to get involved in the student ministry. As you begin to see yourself as a servant, it will change your mindset that a ministry does not exist to serve you but for you to give through serving. When you add the self-directed aspect, you see a disciple in action. Many will serve if asked for a specific task at a particular time; however, an ongoing servant who is self-directed does not have to be prodded to get involved or sign up. They are there and willing. Motivation should naturally come from walking with Christ, and as the servant is being transformed, then they want to be engaged in the work. Motivation naturally comes from within when someone desires to be a part of the church. You have observed a student or adult who just desires to be present and involved and the refreshing spirit they bring to the people around them.

PAUSE & REFLECT

1. What is your motivation in your weekly rhythm?
2. How do you view your ability to be self-directed in your service?

SELF-DIRECTED, MOTIVATED MIDDLE SCHOOLERS

The impacts of being self-directed or motivated in learning have been explored through research[6] on leadership and self-efficacy scores.[7] The idea of a self-directed learner has been around since the 1960s. It is a goal for college graduates to be self-directed learners by the time they complete their degree so they can be ready as self-motivated workers. The self-directed learner will figure out solutions and thus be motivated to complete their work. The ongoing focus of the research on being a self-directed learner and a self-motivated worker has been on this. The focus of self-directed learning may need to be considered in your training with students, but being a self-directed person is more than the focus on how the student learns. Although adults can benefit from understanding skill development through self-directed learning in middle school, the goal of self-directed learning culminates in emerging adulthood. The harder component to achieve is helping a middle schooler become self-motivated to accomplish their work at school, church, or at home.

Discipleship with middle schoolers allows for the development of life skills such as self-control and self-regulating behavior. We have the teaching of the fruit of the spirit to encourage how we need to be people who show the outside world the difference Christ makes within us. If you talk with an elementary or secondary teacher, they might share with you the importance of the development of skills through self-directed extracurricular activities with the arts or sports to help students develop their skills. I believe the youth group is the best place to help students develop their skills in spiritual, character, and interpersonal formation. When you consider the life-long impact of helping middle school students to become self-directed in their spiritual formation, not just in their school work, then a big picture of developing students is paramount to youth ministry. This motivation should carry on into high school as they continue to grow. For example, a middle school student relies on someone to drive them and help them with their basic needs as they continue to develop,

---

[6] https://pmc.ncbi.nlm.nih.gov/articles/PMC7159015/
[7] https://digitalcommons.liberty.edu/doctoral/4776/

which can cause them to be less motivated since they are reliant on others still for several aspects of life.

SELF-DIRECTED, MOTIVATED HIGH SCHOOLERS
The self-directed high school student should be thriving in their school work as they continue to be motivated to further develop their abilities. They are experiencing accomplishments in their respective sports or other extracurricular activities. As they begin to discover success, it will fuel their motivation to achieve more and become more self-directed in their development. A self-directed middle school student could exist in some areas of their life. They may be focused on their school work but forget to do their chores, whereas high school students can begin to show a self-directed life in all areas. Older high school students should become more self-directed as they prepare for what is next in the college or vocational pathway.

High school students will be driven toward learning to be self-directed learners, which should cause student leaders to pause and wonder how to create self-directed options for the student's spiritual formation. Motivation is one aspect that can drive the student toward becoming a self-directed disciple who begins to take ownership of their maturing faith. Adults sometimes think a high school student's self-motivation is more like pushing a rope. The student, some days or weeks, is not motivated but other times demonstrates great self-motivation. The process for high school is one of many highs and lows, and if we can help them become self-directed and self-motivated in their connectivity to Christ and His Church, it will be a great step toward their emerging adult stage.

SELF-DIRECTED, MOTIVATED EMERGING ADULTS
The transition from having ongoing daily instruction that encourages self-directed skills on your education journey shifts to being self-directed with the teacher influencing at a distance more than hands-on coaching. College is the place where the pace and completion of assignments and progress for the student in their studies is more self-directed than teacher-directed. The ownership that this stage requires is enormous for becoming a lifelong self-directed learner. This translates well for the disciple in their self-directed engagement with the spiritual disciplines for their spiritual formation. Emerging into adulthood shifts the ownership more to the student. This happens in the church as well, and young adult ministry is more self-directed than student ministry from their high school experience.

Emerging adults can make adjustments to becoming fully devoted, self-directed followers of Christ. They are also making adjustments in learning to be self-motivated and continue to be involved in the local church. Serving in a ministry can help emerging adults be self-directed as they assist in teaching or other ministry preparation. They may have to agree to a moral covenant for serving and thus create some accountability or self-motivation in their weekly rhythm of life. Student ministry leaders need to help emerging adults become more self-directed as they deal with the changing landscape of life post-high school. Emerging adults may struggle with adjusting to all the ways they need to be self-motivated, and the church can help them find a place to belong as they mature in life. Adults become peers or guides, especially those that are in the next phase that the young adults will be maturing into.

SELF-DIRECTED MOTIVATED ADULTS
Adults can be like students and find themselves to be self-directed at work or at home, but church is less of an area where they are self-directed and need more encouragement to be faithful to their commitments. You can understand this when an adult is serving in an area outside of their giftedness or comfort zone, but the challenge is to know each adult and what their self-directed motivation ability is to coach them well. Adults have been moving more and more toward being self-directed individuals in all areas of their lives since they were students. The temptation for adults is to not be patient with students who are early on in their process of becoming self-directed in life. Responsibilities that adults have to balance can cause them to feel a need to take a break on the weekend or after a long day of work. In student ministry, we have to help adults address being self-motivated in their ministry responsibilities in addition to their normal adult weekly routines.

This does not mean that if you struggle to be a self-directed disciple, you are less than those who are self-directed. The disciples struggled with Jesus to be self-directed, and He continued to pour into them so they could become more self-directed in their ministry. If we struggle in this area, then thankfully, we can lean into becoming more self-directed and be a more engaged servant in the church. Motivation is an area that can be harder to cultivate because our motivation has to come from within. When you consider the full counsel of Scripture, you will find many verses that can be considered motivational. A motivated follower of Christ finds it within to serve the Lord. Here are a few verses of encouragement for you to consider.

> [4] Rejoice in the Lord always; again I will say, rejoice. [5] Let your reasonableness be known to everyone. The Lord is at hand; [6] do not be anxious about anything, but in everything by prayer and supplication with thanksgiving let

your requests be made known to God. [7] And the peace of God, which surpasses all understanding, will guard your hearts and your minds in Christ Jesus.
— Philippians 4:4-7

[6] Humble yourselves, therefore, under the mighty hand of God so that at the proper time he may exalt you, [7] casting all your anxieties on him, because he cares for you.
—1 Peter 5:6-7

QUESTIONS TO CONSIDER

1. Brainstorm with different ages in the student ministry leadership to discuss how to be a self-directed, motivated servant in your church.

2. What did you learn about other leaders and how they are self-directed but different from your approach to being self-directed?

3. Who is someone who models this well? How so? How can you help other students and leaders become more self-directed in their participation and walk with the Lord?

CHAPTER 8
MINDSET OF A SERVANT

A volunteer who grows spiritually is the assumption for people who serve. The passion to walk with the Lord each day is needed.

> [1] I appeal to you therefore, brothers, by the mercies of God, to present your bodies as a living sacrifice, holy and acceptable to God, which is your spiritual worship. [2] Do not be conformed to this world, but be transformed by the renewal of your mind, that by testing you may discern what is the will of God, what is good and acceptable and perfect.
> — Romans 12:1-2

In the previous chapter, we reviewed the concept of being self-directed, motivated servants. This concept is only achievable when the servant has the right mindset. We get the opportunity to renew our minds each day to be like Christ.

Consider those two powerful verses from Paul. The call to present ourselves as a living sacrifice. The servant is focused on becoming more like Christ in the pursuit of pleasing God and becoming holy. This process is not simple; it is a training for the people in youth ministry and an ongoing development of the mind of Christ. This mindset will keep those serving to model the call to servanthood that Jesus challenged the first disciples to consider. A lifestyle of serving others is not unique to Christianity, as many people will serve in their community or volunteer in various ways in organizations. The spiritual growth aspect, combined with serving, is what sets this concept apart from others who serve in our world. In Paul's writing, the understanding of faith and works together come to reveal how we can develop the mindset to serve Christ and His Church faithfully.

Spiritual growth must be evidenced by the team members. Often, we take the person's willingness to serve without thinking through how the team member could be discipled to serve. Linking together with other believers to serve in the local church should be one of the strongest aspects of our growth. When you combine spiritual habits to grow toward Christlikeness, then we should naturally want to be with God's people in His Church. We then combine the personal and corporate disciplines together with serving by utilizing our giftedness, and we have the best blend to be disciples who make disciples.

You may have observed a volunteer or staff member who was always complaining or serving as if it was a burden to their life. The person who serves out of obligation or guilt does not display a servant who is molded by Christ. A person serving out of this type of posture will struggle to grow and will usually not have the demeanor of a servant. The growth as we serve should be from a motivation to be more like Christ by being on the team so that they can be nurtured spiritually. I observed a leader recently who constantly circled back to encourage or speak truth to others. She was an inspiration who, through her service, demonstrated to others how they could serve by encouraging others. This is the level of growth we need.

PAUSE & REFLECT

What are you doing to keep the mindset of a servant? Are you someone who serves with joy, or do you find yourself serving out of guilt?

The natural position in the culture is to think of yourself first. When this is the mindset, then the people believe an organization exists to support or serve them. The Church provides a different perspective as Christ modeled the posture of serving without the expectation of being served. The posture of being available to serve comes from your heart to your mind, and it moves toward being a servant. A servant having this mindset is one of the ministry challenges that has to be overcome in developing the mindset of the people.

HOW CAN MIDDLE SCHOOL STUDENTS MODEL SERVANTHOOD?

A middle school student has the capacity to be a servant and model the characteristics of servanthood in their lives. Children begin to take on responsibilities as they age; they have extracurricular activities and academic achievements that together help them mature as people. As their personality develops, these achievements can cause them to be conceited, arrogant, or humble. The youth group is one place that can help them understand the role of servanthood and how to be a humble individual who serves well within their church. They can learn the lifelong trait of the need to serve even when no recognition is offered, but rather from a heart that desires to serve.

HOW CAN HIGH SCHOOL STUDENTS MODEL SERVANTHOOD?

Middle school is a transition from childhood, but the transition from middle to high school is one in which the student continues to earn more independence. As they mature, they begin to develop their skills and interests toward a career. Some begin to work, take on leadership responsibilities, and have opportunities to serve others as they pursue their high school diploma. The student ministry can provide for high schoolers to develop a mindset of servanthood in every area of their life. The high school years offer a unique opportunity to help build lifelong, servant-minded people. It is beneficial to give high school students opportunities to serve and be mentored in the pathway of servanthood. They should have moments of wrestling between the desire to be recognized for achievement and the struggle to press on when not even a compliment is offered for the work performed.

HOW CAN EMERGING ADULTS MODEL SERVANTHOOD?

Emerging adults have been battling it out to survive high school and be found on the other side in vocational school or college, preparing for the next season of their journey. It is a challenging time to navigate, find your place in this world, stay true to what you have been taught, and believe as a servant of Christ. The world continues to press that servanthood is not the pathway for a rising adult who desires to achieve in their career and life. The current Western culture encourages delaying marriage or having children to pursue life, accomplishment, and adventure. A natural pull toward selfish desires and focus places the emerging adult in a struggle to deny self and follow Christ. This reminds us of the disciples that Christ first called to follow Him as their teacher and how they denied their career paths and followed Jesus. The world requires grit from the student, whatever season of their quest to figure out life.

HOW CAN ADULTS MODEL SERVANTHOOD?

Adults set the climate for how students perceive the world, including the servant leader. Parents and student ministry leaders will determine if the students have a mindset in their homes of entitlement or one of servanthood. Consider adults who have influenced your mindset of being a servant of the Lord. What did you notice in them that drew you to be a servant like them? Adults who continue to sacrifice for the next generation are a special group of servants. They have many places where they could invest their life, but they have chosen to be faithful to reach students and serve in this vital area of the church.

Adults have an influence on students and also other adults. When you consider the impact of modeling servanthood that the adults in the congregation can make on their peers, the ability to recruit volunteers is more organic for the student ministry leader to cultivate. We see other adults serving, and the lifestyle and posture of the leadership are observed, causing people to realize that they have the capacity to serve as well. Influence, mentorship, and modeling by encouraging other adults to have the mindset of a servant.

QUESTIONS TO CONSIDER

1. What is your definition of a servant?

2. How do you currently model the mindset of a servant in your life?

3. What adjustments could you make to increase your servant life focus?

In Mark 10:42-45, James and John questioned Jesus about being able to sit at Jesus' right and left.

> "[42] And Jesus called them to him and said to them, 'You know that those who are considered rulers of the Gentiles lord it over them, and their great ones exercise authority over them. [43] But it shall not be so among you. But whoever would be great among you must be your servant, [44] and whoever would be first among you must be slave of all. [45] For even the Son of Man came not to be served but to serve, and to give his life as a ransom for many.'"
> — Mark 10:42-45

Jesus reminded the disciples and us to model being a servant by serving others. I pray that you will be a humble servant in each area of your life, including your role in student ministry.

CHAPTER 9
ENGAGED IN THE LOCAL CHURCH

A team member, whether paid or volunteer, needs to be engaged in their church. You may have observed a person who is willing to work hard in the auxiliary aspects of ministry but never engages in worship. They will be the first to clean up the kitchen, serve on the safety team, or be a greeter, but they struggle with engaging in the deeper ministries of the church. A willingness to serve needs to be shepherded with a balance of personal engagement to their spiritual formation and nurture within the ongoing ministries of the church. Many times, availability wins the day, and the time serving in auxiliary monopolies is a volunteer or staff member's time on Sunday or mid-week gatherings.

A Scriptural foundation for balance needs to be more precise in terms of how much we serve and how much time is required in order to abide in Christ. In Acts 2:42-47, we see the early church devoted itself to being together in the work, which included ministry, teaching, prayer, worship, and fellowship. In student ministry, it is important to gauge how the team members are doing in terms of their balance of serving and abiding. Burnout has arisen as a common theme in society as people are pushed to the brink of their education, family, career, or job, to name just a few areas. As we see the shift also to include ministry burnout, the need to engage with other believers and the church and not just show up to deplete a person's resource through serving is crucial in maintaining a healthy team of people invested in student ministry.

This season of life has been part of the "Great Resignation" that is happening in our society. Following the COVID-19 pandemic, volunteer resignations set off a turnover in the job market. The reasons were numerous, with low pay, feeling disrespected, childcare challenges, not enough hours scheduled, not enough flexibility, or desire to relocate were a few of the reasons.[8] Data reveals this trend has already been occurring for at least a decade and is only growing, and some researchers link this to the five "R's:" retirement, relocation, reconsideration, reshuffling, and reluctance.[9] The "Great Resignation" spurred the younger generation to see older siblings, parents, and mentors make life choices during this period, which caused them to pause and consider their next steps. Students observe this and ask questions about what to do with their future. They need to see a student ministry team of people who love the Lord and His Church. They need to understand what it means to be engaged in the work of the Church for a lifetime and not just a season. Gentelligence, as we discussed in Chapter 2, helps the generations learn from one another. The generational impact of an intergenerational workforce will help cultivate student relationships within the church.

PAUSE & REFLECT

Stop and read Acts 2:42-47. What stands out to you from the early church? Would you consider yourself to be engaged in the local church like those from Acts 2? Why or why not?

STUDENTS AS AN EXAMPLE OF ENGAGEMENT

Unfortunately, during a team member's stint of service, there may be a time where that team member is not fully engaged in church. Tithing, worshipping, discipling, and serving are the four ways that I believe we can observe engagement. Students can be involved in the local church through giving, worship, discipleship, and serving in ministry. Students who have income through allowance or employment can actively participate. Think of students who showed up when a need was mentioned or a special mission emphasis was placed on them. I have seen students give generously to a food drive or mission need or fill a shoebox for Christmas with a Samaritan's Purse. They may give from their parent's resources, but they have the ability to participate in the work. The entire congregation can be influenced by their genuine worship and how they participate in the corporate gathering. Active involvement in being discipled and engaging in clubs and school organizations, as well as the student ministry, is needed to disciple other teenagers.

---

[8] https://www.pewresearch.org/short-reads/2022/03/09/majority-of-workers-who-quit-a-job-in-2021-cite-low-pay-no-opportunities-for-advancement-feeling-disrespected/
[9] https://hbr.org/2022/03/the-great-resignation-didnt-start-with-the-pandemic

EMERGING ADULTS AS AN EXAMPLE OF ENGAGEMENT
Young adults living for Christ impact those students who look up to them and the adults who are older than them. When college students come to lead a retreat weekend or serve on the staff of a camp, the students attend, and the young adults become the next phase of a committed believer that students are grappling to understand and ultimately embrace. The young adult season is one of struggle to find your way in giving, being engaged in the local church through worship, being active in discipleship, and serving within the church. Many college students engage in campus ministry, which provides an opportunity for many aspects of the local church, such as worship, discipleship, and opportunities to serve in missions and ministry. I have served as a campus minister and believe strongly in engaging campuses for Christ. The connection on a college campus to the local church is key. The student ministry operates within the context of the local church, and we have to remember that an intergenerational church is where we should engage our lives with other believers as well as with ministries that reinforce the work of the local church. The love we have for our area of ministry should not be divorced from our connection to being faithful to a local church. Student ministry has a great responsibility to engage middle school, high school, and college students in a local church.

As a student, I was involved in my student ministry as a middle school and high school student. As an adult, I've served as a paid student ministry staff member and an adult volunteer leader. While reflecting on my different seasons in student ministry, I've been inspired because students, emerging adults, and adults of all ages have encouraged my devotion, development, and discipleship. Being engaged within the church and its ministries cannot be overstated for those of us who serve at all ages. As you recall from chapter five, our giftedness is needed within the church. That giftedness is not realized to its full potential without our full engagement as a student, emerging adults, or an adult of any age. Think of a sporting event for middle school, high school, and college. Now, reflect on the student section. Each sporting event for student-athletes with a student section is for fans who are engaged in their school and desire to be there. Imagine your local church and encourage the students to be engaged in the student section for Christ.

ADULTS AS AN EXAMPLE OF ENGAGEMENT
Do you ever pay close attention to the student section at a college football game? A thermometer for crowd engagement and setting the tone of the fans in the crowd. However, working adults will make up the bulk of the stadium at a sporting event even though students primarily bring the energy. A few action steps to help you as a leader know you help set the tone in your ministry with your example.

ACTION STEPS
1. Consistently attend a corporate intergenerational worship service

2. Faithfully contribute to your youth ministry.

3. Give of your time, talent, and treasure through your church.

4. Find a couple of people with whom you can keep each other accountable to stay engaged in the church.

I have had team members who have not been faithfully engaged in tithing. This is unfortunate when a paid staff member or volunteer withholds giving back a portion of their resources to the work. Usually, we addressed this accountability by turning in names to the financial team member of the church who could verify the potential team list for giving. We can observe attendance to worship. I have had student ministry small group leaders, chaperones, and other volunteers who did not consistently attend worship. Some even attended other churches for worship as they were unhappy with an aspect of the church but desired to still serve in student ministry. Being engaged in the local church you serve is a key aspect of modeling engagement for the teenagers of the church.

Letting a team member go for not being engaged is one of the hardest aspects of being a team leader. Some church members like to treat church more like free agency in sports teams than being committed to a church as a faithful team member. However, if you are going to have standards for being engaged in the church, those need to be a part of the position description so people are aware of the expectations when they are being recruited to join the team. As we discussed in previous chapters, the team members need to be engaged in being mentored and discipled to walk with Christ. I serve at a seminary, and our mission statement reminds me of this truth each week: "We prepare servants to walk with Christ, proclaim His truth, and fulfill His mission." I believe that is the mission of the team leader to prepare the team members to walk with Christ, proclaim His truth, and fulfill His mission." Walking with Christ is a key part of being engaged in ministry.

CONSIDERATIONS FOR ENGAGEMENT
What level of engagement do you have with the church? Do you rank more like a fair-weather fan of a college sports team or a devoted no matter how good or bad the season that is your school, and you wear their colors and still show up? When we ponder being an engaged servant within the student ministry, we should be fully devoted members.

We should not be fair-weathered based on who is there, how we score the leadership, or how we feel we are being served. Devotion should be a natural desire to be around the people of God and grow through serving, giving, worshipping, and discipling others around us.

QUESTIONS TO CONSIDER

1. What does your church consider an engaged member to be in the overall work of the church?

2. Do you struggle to be engaged in your local church? Why?

3. How does being engaged in the church encourage your walk with Christ?

4. Where can you demonstrate a more engaged church member?

CHAPTER 10
UNDERSTANDING OF YOUTH CULTURE

Student ministry is an evolving process of understanding each generation. Many leading voices have helped us in student ministry to have a better grasp of the current culture of teenagers. The aspect that can be a struggle for youth ministry leaders is to chase what is popular in the larger culture to attract students or follow the cultural fads of teenagers, which can be a challenge in student ministry. A foundational understanding of the impacts of youth culture and the developmental components of creating a student ministry culture that helps students connect with Christ and His Church is key.

What defines culture in your community? The internet has brought the influence of the world into people's homes and even into their hands through a smartphone. The middle school guy on his gaming console has access like the emerging adult in their dorm room on their Mac or the senior adult man with a Smart TV in his home. The culture has now leveled the information and influence from outside perspectives. The ability to navigate the influences and overload of information now challenges the culture from the rural farm to the urban apartment, the metropolitan city, or the small town. The culture of your community is one factor, the online cultural influences on students are another factor, and the culture that is cultivated around students is the other consideration. Think about how each generation has expressed themselves and connected to movements in the world, from protests to causes that motivated action.

PERSPECTIVE
From students to senior adults, each generation experiences cultural influences in their lives. Each generation has its own twist on youth culture, from fashion, music, interests, and leadership style. If you reflect on several

decades, you will smile as the trends in youth culture resurface. Adults did not think bell bottoms of the 70s or large eyeglasses of the 80s would return, but they have ty-dyed t-shirts as well. Classic rock continues to be sung as some of the timeless are discovered by each generation and enjoy some of the same music. Some aspects cause you to shake your head. The "Swifties" of the youth culture is almost like a cult following as students just stand in the parking lot of a Taylor Swift concert if they cannot afford it or do not get tickets through a ticket lottery for one of her shows. Before too many adults joined the bandwagon, I could not believe it, but the older adults did have Woodstock. The 70s also produced the need for stronger youth ministries in the local churches as we see the Jesus movement provide a revival generation for young people to turn to Christ. This revolutionized the local church and even impacted worship style and the need for children and youth ministry through a different lens. You see a pivot that created a launching pad for many ministries in the late 70s and into the 80s as Baby Boomers continued to have children and the youth population began to impact the spending patterns of adults and the youth culture could even impact the economy with fast food choices and entertainment options.

LOCATION, LOCATION, LOCATION

Where you live does impact the culture around you. As teenagers, the culture of a small town where you gather in town, drive up and down the town, and gather in a parking lot is different from the life of a teenager in the metro area. Crime, gang activity, and drugs are a few of the negative influences of youth culture that adolescents can encounter in their community. These factors can be found online or in-person at school or sometimes from within the church. I will spare you the stories from small towns, metro urban environments, or suburban areas, but each has had a negative influence on students that influenced student ministry.

FAMILY MATTERS

Each student is influenced by their family. The influence of family has the greatest impact on students, and it can be positive or negative in the teenager's development. A teenager who has to deal with an absent parent, especially the father, causes issues within the student with a greater risk of suicide, incarceration, drug use, and being a high school dropout. The Center for Fathering unpacks many aspects of the negative impact of a community from fatherless homes and the next generation.[10] The Bible informs us in Proverbs 4 of the needed instruction from parents to be careful with the culture and guard the influences you allow into your life.

---

[10] https://fathers.com/

SOCIO-ECONOMIC FACTORS
Poverty or wealth influences a teenager's experience with culture. Clothing, travel, where you live, what you drive, or how you interact with peers based on how you perceive your status influence how you interact with the culture or respond to its influence.

In student ministry, the struggle is to navigate cultural influences because some students are sheltered from many of the influences outside of their families. Some students come from fractured homes that have resulted in negative cultural interactions that cause a divide among the sheltered kids. Then you have the kids who were just raised in a middle-class family. The factors of culture are influences that students, parents, and youth leaders need to be equipped to navigate culture in redemptive ways.

PAUSE & REFLECT

As you are reading, reflect on the youth culture in your youth group. Pray for specific students that you know are struggling and write their names down. Take time to pray for Godly influences in your students. As you journal and pray, spend time asking the Lord to cleanse you of negative cultural influences. Now, spend some time reflecting on the influences in your life. Do you have any influences that need to be diminished or eliminated? How could you create a margin in your life for stronger Christian influences in your media, friends, and community?

Understanding and navigating youth culture are worthy undertakings, but one that may not be considered is the culture that youth ministry creates among its students.

HOW DO YOU DEVELOP CULTURE IN YOUR MINISTRY?
A healthy youth ministry will have a culture where students want to be there. Students have a good level of discernment when distinguishing those who are genuine in their leadership. Teenagers have a desire for authentic community with one another and adult mentors. The youth ministry that has a great group of adult volunteers who desire to be there will go a long way in establishing a youth culture where students desire to

be present. One consideration for leadership is to make sure the students know about the adult care that is provided by the youth ministry. Another factor for teenagers would be whether they can find a peer community within the student ministry. Not all students will be close friends, but the students have relationships to the extent they desire to be a part of the youth group through their web of relationships.

You want a youth ministry that cultivates a culture where the students find community with peers and adults. Another aspect of the culture can depend on the church's support to support the youth ministry. The overall church supports the students and the youth ministry holistically with staffing, financing, and the needed physical resources. A student ministry that is well supported by the church has the resources needed to cultivate a healthy youth culture within the student ministry. The needed people, space, and physical resources allow the focus on cultivating students to walk with Christ and make Him known.

Families of students impact the youth culture within the student ministry as much as anything else. Each group of students has unique challenges based on their personal, family, and school experiences. The overall support from a mother and father in a loving Christian home cannot be substituted. Many students do not have their parents as advocates or sometimes do not live in the same household. Parentless spiritual formation is a commonplace reality in many youth ministries. Absentee spiritual parents are not discussed as much as other youth culture factors but are the silent largest contributor to the culture within your family structure of student ministry. Youth ministry is more challenging when you do not have the student family involvement and support in what you are trying to accomplish week in and week out.

Each year, the outside influences seem to get louder, or maybe it is just the adult aging process that causes us to be more aware of what influences us. How often do you touch your smartphone, and what would you do with the time if you removed yourself from the attachment? How much time is spent on online gaming, shopping, or streaming? The online impact is influencing teenagers and adults more and more. We have to pause, fast, and reflect on the cultural implications of technology as well as the other factors so we know what is truly influencing us and those around us. Jesus told the disciples, "Behold, I am sending you out as sheep in the midst of wolves, so be wise as serpents and innocent as doves." (Matthew 10:16). He wanted them to be aware of the culture and the people who would try to harm them as they were trying to minister to the people. We may not have the same conditions around us, but we do have to be wise in our surroundings and conduct ourselves with the highest level of purity and innocence as we interact with the world.

QUESTIONS TO CONSIDER

1. Discuss what cultural impacts are the greatest influencers among your student ministry. Socio-economic factors, family matters, location, or greater community influences...

2. What factors are influencing the youth culture in student ministry: peer connections, adult involvement, church support, or absentee spiritual parents?

3. Do you consider aspects of youth culture throughout the year? If so, how do you gauge the various influences and aspects of teenagers and their families?

PART 3

HOW

The section you may have wanted to unpack from the start is how to serve as a team in student ministry. Before getting to the nuts and bolts of how to function within student ministry as a team, it was important to cultivate the understanding of why we invest our lives into the next generation for Christ and who should be a part of the ministry to reach the student generation of the day through your church. Now, we will spend some time looking at some of the practical aspects of serving together in this work.

CHAPTER 11
VOLUNTEERS AS A T.E.A.M.

Putting pieces together in a ministry can sometimes feel like a Lego set without the instructions. Four things can be derived from how to build a team with your volunteer workforce. When I begin to think of the word team, I like the following acronym: A person on the team who is teachable. A person who is willing to be engaged in the student ministry and be a hard worker does not just want to hang around the student ministry. The person is available to serve and has the right attitude for being a part of a winning team. The team member needs to be ministry-minded. A person who does not lose interest or focus on the work by being around students and their families and ministering to them and their needs. Let's take a few moments and dive into the idea of volunteering in student ministry as a T.E.A.M.

TEACHABLE

Experts seem to abound on the internet. You can find a how-to video for almost anything from cooking, making a repair on your home, a DIY project, or schoolwork, names just a few categories. I am constantly relying on someone to teach me about something. When gardening, I search for answers about a bug, planting solutions, or even when to plant. How to rebind a Bible was another interesting topic. I watched the video and ordered the supplies on Amazon.

Imagine Bill is someone you inherited on your team, and he is open to new ways of doing some things, but he has some aspects that make him stuck in his ways of doing things. It is hard to penetrate those areas of Bill's life to be teachable and learn that how you approach students or how you interact has more options than you have considered. Bill operates from a posture of if it is not broken, then don't worry about it. Unlike Bill, Francis is someone you recruited and are excited about getting rolling as a new team member. You recruited Francis because she is open to learning new ways and techniques to engage students, but her struggle is being teachable that some new process for events should be followed. Then you have Kyle, who is a great student but comes from a very involved family that has been in the church for years. He is dedicated but has tendencies to rely on the family name and influence more than being teachable at times. You get the concept of how different people are teachable in some areas or in some ways and how to begin to consider if you are a partially teachable team member or a teachable person 100% of the time in every area.

Think about your experiences with searching for a YouTube Reel to help you with something or to teach you about a subject matter. How do you interact with letting other people speak into your life, whether in-person or online? Do you have standards for who gets to teach you? In life, we have teachers who are sometimes chosen for us or a person in leadership above us who teaches. In being teachable, you are open to others speaking truth into your life, such as parents, peers, mentors, leaders, coaches, and sometimes from a person you did not expect. In every student ministry, I have been blessed to serve students, parents, volunteers, and church members who have taught me in various ways. Early on, I was not as teachable because I thought I knew more than I did or people would compliment me on my work, and over time, the Lord has allowed me to see the need to remain teachable as I mature in my relationship with Him.

PAUSE & REFLECT

Take a moment and list some ways you are teachable in your ministry. If you are comfortable sharing with other team members, learn from each other about being open to people speaking truth into your life and ministry.

ENGAGED

In hurricane prep before the storm, it is common to put sandbags out in areas where you don't want to have water intrusion in a business or home. Teams of people will come together. Usually, neighbors help neighbors, co-workers, and friends to make sure each household is ready for the storm. After the storm passes then, they engage in helping each other clean up and recover. You can make several connections to a ministry team from this example, but imagine the volunteer workforce coming together with an all-hands-on-deck mindset that we must get the work accomplished, and time is of the essence. This is not a team effort when we get around to it. If our worldview indicates the Gospel changes lives, then students and families need the team to be fully engaged in the work.

PAUSE & REFLECT

Write a brief description of what it means to be a totally engaged team member in your student ministry.

Many people think of a couple that is reaching the milestone in their relationship of realizing that they will get married and enter an engagement period. This usually has photos, people, and a ring, but the one factor is the commitment toward the marriage, which is that you will be committed to the person and promise to marry them. This means during the engagement, you are working on the relationship, preparing to be married, and planning your wedding. Think about serving on a ministry team you have committed to serve and, as a result, are to be engaged in that work. Since you are in this committed relationship, then you have agreed to work on yourself, prepare for your ministry assignments, and plan for the ministry so that you will be a faithful, engaged team member. Different seasons of our lives can cause us to be less engaged in the work of the ministry. If you begin to notice the commitment waning among team members, then have a conversation about life with them. You may discover something is going on in their life that you were not aware of, and you can pray for them or offer to lighten their load. If someone has been a great team member and has begun to be less engaged, then moving them to a different place may cause them to reengage, but you will want to discuss this with the team member first.

AVAILABLE

Being fully engaged requires the team members to make themselves available for the work. Everyone is busy, and each person has other responsibilities, so within the parameters available means not having to be coerced, begged, or cajoled to show up and be available for your part on the team. Could you imagine the football team if the offensive coordinator just took a day for himself and was not available for gameday or the quarterback not being at practice because he had homework? It is interesting how, in some places in our lives, no excuses matter, but in the church, people put their availability in when convenient or in parentheses (if nothing comes up, I will be there). Think about the people that serve them and what kind of availability mindset they operate from.

PAUSE & REFLECT

Personally, what mindset do you have about being available for the team you serve on?

I think of the parable of the good Samaritan when I ponder being available to serve. Different people passed by with the capacity to help but chose not to help. I desire to be a team member who is available like a good Samaritan to serve the needs as they arise and offer to serve. We have many life situations that can limit us for good reasons, but being a person that the team can count on to be there and pitch in during intense busy seasons as needed is an important consideration for being a team member.

let people know I'm available

A teachable, engaged, and available team member are great characteristics for a volunteer, but without a mindset for ministry, this would only produce a person hungry to serve who is growing, and although they are committed to the team and present can be a challenge to be an asset to the work unless an understanding for the ministry exists.

MINISTRY MINDED

A person being willing to volunteer and serve on a team is not synonymous with each other. Being a team member takes more commitment than just volunteering for a position, task, or event. Consider Jeff. He can volunteer for one fall retreat and help with the food. It only requires a little shopping, one weekend, and interacting and serving students food. This requires no training on his part, and all Jeff must do is pass a background check. This option to be a part of serving the youth ministry of the church is different than joining the youth ministry, which is a weekly ongoing ministry team. Jeff needs to have training, weekly ministry assignments, and ongoing interaction with students throughout the year. He would need to arrive early and leave later for assigned ministry times. He should prepare his heart spiritually before arriving at church to serve. Jeff should desire to learn students' names and learn what they are interested in, and over time, they begin to understand they can count on Jeff as more than someone who occasionally shows

up in the youth ministry space. Jeff can still play an important role by supporting the work of youth ministry through being in a supporting role with food for events or logistical needs in coordinating the work.

PAUSE & REFLECT

Read Philippians 2:2-4 and write down some thoughts about having an "others" people mindset through serving as part of a bigger team for ministry.

A person who is focused on ministry is willing to look out for the interests of others and not just their needs or those in their immediate family. Paul wrote to those in Philippi to have the mind to look out for the interests of others. A volunteer or staff member should be willing to have a "T.E.A.M." focus on their service.

QUESTIONS TO CONSIDER

1. Consider your definition of a team. How is it different from being teachable, engaged, available, and ministry-minded?

2. What are the barriers that you encounter in trying to be a unified team in your student ministry?

3. How can you work with others to improve your team?

CHAPTER 12
COMMUNICATION

Do you hear me? Hello... How many times do I have to tell you?

You are so clueless! Why don't you understand me?

Chat, snap, text; we have many ways to communicate without speaking. Digital means have extended the ability to stay in touch, connect, or receive/send information 24/7. You have seen it at a table of people at a restaurant, and everyone is on a device. Some restaurants provide gaming devices at the table to make entertaining yourself over talking with people possible. Students tend to want to be on their devices even when together. Some families do not allow technology for various reasons, which creates variances in how students communicate. Online gaming has created the ability for guys to talk more than ever imagined as they are connected, talking through their quests to conquer one scene after another in the hope of world domination in a game. You have varying thoughts about technology, but the bigger issue is how we communicate with each other. Different ages utilize language in different ways as they seek to understand the world and navigate their journey. The quest to understand middle school may never be solved, but in high school, emerging adults and adults begin to have a deeper meaning with each other as they see to have a lifelong relationship and not just survive their day.

The struggle to navigate the overload of information to arrive at the ability to discern and communicate with each other is a challenge. We are processing many things at once and, at times, halfway focused on a conversation. As a dad, it is common for me to be engrossed in something and not fully hear a family member in the same room as me. It is not intentional, but the background noise does not always allow for focus. The observance of a middle schooler aggravating their older sibling, the high schooler who is compassionate to a younger child, and the adult who stops and just listens to the teenager's troubles are moments when we realize how powerful our words and actions are to other people. You have been shopping or at an event and observe people's interactions with each other. Some of these interactions cause you to smile as you see a new couple in love, holding hands, and just enjoying the presence of the other. Another glance and you see a parent and child enraged with one another over an item of clothing that the mom is just not approving for her daughter, and you see the worst of communication as people have their moments. You pass the food court, and an older gentleman is just upset over the amount of food for the price on his plate, and he just loses his temper with the unfortunate worker at the counter. As you have some life examples of positive and negative communication, we will consider various groups or people we communicate with within the student ministry.

COMMUNICATION WITH STUDENTS

Language, empathy, understanding, meaning of expression, clarity, information, knowledge, and wisdom are just some ways communication can be interpreted. In youth ministry, it is vital that the truths of God's Word and how to be the Church are communicated at the level students can interpret and understand. Serving students well by knowing how to communicate with them, as well as teaching them to communicate with peers and other age groups and authority groups within their lives, is crucial for their overall spiritual development. Consider the tone of voice and body language as you communicate with students. You may utilize language that does not connect or dismiss an issue that is of great importance to them, but you do not consider an issue at all.

Proverbs 18 has insight for each person to consider what they say and even how quickly they speak.

In verse 2, "A fool takes no pleasure in understanding, but only in expressing his opinion."

If you are always talking, then your communication is limited.

In verse 4, "The words of a man's mouth are deep waters; the fountain of wisdom is a bubbling brook."

The words you speak are impactful and should be weighed before you tear people down or build them up.

In verses 6 through 8, "[6] A fool's lips walk into a fight, and his mouth invites a beating. [7] A fool's mouth is his ruin, and his lips are a snare to his soul. [8] The words of a whisperer are like delicious morsels; they go down into the inner parts of the body."

Your communication can create much grief or cause deep trouble for others, so be careful with how you speak.

In verse 13, "If one gives an answer before he hears, it is his folly and shame."

Each of us should work to listen more.

In verse 15, "An intelligent heart acquires knowledge, and the ear of the wise seeks knowledge."

In verse 17, "The one who states his case first seems right, until the other comes and examines him."

You don't always have to be the first to present your side.

In verses 20 and 21, "[20] From the fruit of a man's mouth his stomach is satisfied; he is satisfied by the yield of his lips. [21] Death and life are in the power of the tongue, and those who love it will eat its fruits."

Your overall well-being in mind, body, soul, and strength can be impacted by your communication. Proverbs 18 gives a perspective that can apply to students, but it is intended for everyone to understand the power of communication and its impact on ourselves as well as others.

COMMUNICATION WITH PARENTS

In light of the needs of students and other adults in the church, the communication intended for those who are the entrusted guardians of students is special. They are trusting the student ministry to shepherd and protect their student. They expect a high standard of training and equipping the student to interact well with others. Leaders need to understand the language of parents so they can communicate needed information in a manner parents can receive and understand. As a parent, I have seen a coach, teacher, minister, and volunteer at church all lose the trust of people due to their actions. Student ministry leaders need to work to maintain trust in how they communicate, both spoken and through actions, that they are who they say they are and follow through on their commitments. A wise mentor expressed to me early on in my ministry that you never want to lose the trust of those with whom entrusted leadership within the congregation to you. I believe in student ministry, and the trust of families of students are some of the most important people who need to know we care, are available, and understand the struggles they face to follow Christ each week.

COMMUNICATION WITH STAFF/VOLUNTEERS

I was talking with the CEO of a large company that employs several hundred people about the challenges of communicating with staff. A supervisor who can communicate with their team is an important piece in the health of a company. Staff turnover is costly in the corporate world, so the company is trying to limit staff turnover. The ability to communicate with one another on the team will contribute to the health of the student ministry workforce. This level of communication from student ministry leaders will be a model for students' healthy interpersonal communication skills. Staff need to know what is happening, and you will communicate with people each week both verbally and nonverbally. I have learned to improve over the years by looking into a mirror and realizing that I may have an expression that is not friendly or a loud voice that can communicate anger when it is just simply my normal loud self. My speech teacher taught us to practice in front of a full-length mirror to realize these aspects of communication. Over the years, it has helped me improve my ability to communicate with others. We all will still have moments where we are not our best, but if we work on our communication skills, we will improve.

COMMUNICATION WITH SENIOR LEADERSHIP

We all answer to someone, and learning to express ourselves with those who are over us can be a challenge. As you interact with senior leadership, a humble posture should be the default manner in which you address those who are over you. You can present ideas with confidence and defend your area since you are the primary student ministry advocate. A respectful approach to leadership is to let them know you value their position and understand their support is needed and input desired. Being a team player who supports the overall vision and does not talk down about senior leadership with others is an important aspect of having good communication among the larger church leadership. Always strive to be prepared to give updates or account for events or aspects happening in the student ministry to keep senior leadership informed of good things that are happening. Also, be sure they know immediately when struggles or conflicts are happening so they are aware. It is not healthy for senior leadership to be caught off guard by not being in the loop on what is happening within the student ministry. Understand that you may not always be in places where senior leadership needs to know what is happening in the student ministry, so find ways to give a weekly update, whether a weekly email or a brief overview verbally in a meeting, but be sure they know the talking points.

PAUSE & REFLECT

Take a moment and consider your recent words and deeds and how you mark people with those. Do those words and deeds model love and point people toward Christ?

Paul David Tripp writes, "We are born with the need for relationships. Each of our lives is a community project. So, we must always respond to one another with the humble recognition that we need one another. This means responding in ways that strengthen our community, deepen our bonds, and stimulate candid, loving communication."[11] Notice that he does not designate an age group in the challenge in our community project of doing life together. Students, parents, staff and volunteers, and senior leadership within the church community should communicate with the fundamental understanding that we need one another, and this is evidenced by the tone and manner in which we communicate with one another. Two words are needed as evidence from our lives, and they are to love and respect each other.

Parents and teenagers will have moments in their communication when misunderstanding, anger, encouragement, love, kindness, gentleness, and many other emotions can be expressed at times. A pastor was teaching and made the reference that as we do this as parents, we mark our children. The words we use and what we communicate through our actions will mark our teenagers for their lifetime, both positive and negative.

Communication is a powerful instrument that we have, and I am not perfect, and I mess up every week like some of you. I have moments where I like to honk my horn as I drive to remind others of opportunities for improvement in their life. In my home, there are moments when I am tired or stressed, and the words are not encouraging but critical. I have been a team leader, and I was more worried about the results than the health and spiritual development of the team. I share this to remind us that we are

---

[11] https://www.crossway.org/articles/8-ways-we-normalize-the-abnormal/

human and that only with Christ can we communicate the love of Christ. Communication for me is better when it is written in a note, card, or text, but my people still need to hear my voice express words of affirmation, love, joy, and kindness throughout our home and ministry. The struggle is real, and when you are having a good day, your teenager may not be having a good day because schoolwork is not going well, a friend is having a moment, or even the team is a challenge, and the results are not as desired. Frustration can lead to any of us not communicating well and voicing our frustration to someone else. This can be in the home between teenagers and parents, on a team with colleagues, or in the ministry with senior leadership in the church. We are going to spend some time on each of these areas of communication within a student ministry. Students, parents, staff and volunteers, and senior leadership within the church.

QUESTIONS TO CONSIDER

1. Do you think you are an effective communicator?

2. In what ways could you improve how you communicate with students?

3. How could you improve your interpersonal communication with parents?

4. Do you believe you communicate well through digital ways such as email, texting, or social media?

CHAPTER 13
NAVIGATING ISSUES AND CHALLENGES

Ministry always faces challenges, concerns, and difficulties because we are against an enemy that does not want our mission to be successful (John 10:10). These challenges and issues often involve people but can also extend to property, finances, or specific types of programs. We press on and understand that team members, families, teenagers, and church members will face issues and challenges that we must navigate. We cover many of these aspects in our other resource, "Protect." People will always have life issues and challenges that present themselves in the student ministry, so the need to be prepared to address common occurrences such as bullying, girl drama, or a bad breakup of a couple within the students can be understood as challenges that happen with students. The extreme can become online stalking of a bully or the ex-boyfriend that becomes violent after the breakup. These are examples of challenges that can arise among students. Peer-related matters between students are common, and adults need to know the policies and procedures that have been developed to handle issues with people as they arise. A little girl drama at camp, a few middle school boys pulling pranks, a high school bully, or a bad breakup of a couple can all present student issues and challenges that have the capacity to disrupt the ministry.

STUDENT CHALLENGES WITH PEERS

Peer challenges are just one of the struggles with people because you could have volunteer challenges or staff disagreements. If you have been in student ministry for a while, you have your own stories of how students, parents, volunteers, and staff can experience their moments of challenge. You can have a student stop attending because of the girl drama or stay with their parent while at church and not engage in the student ministry.

Parents can sometimes have strong feelings about an issue and invoice another family if something was broken during a youth event in their home. Volunteers can disagree over sleeping accommodations and throw the other adults' bags out on the lawn. Staff can be difficult to work with and challenge your event request or facility needs for an event, causing intense disagreement or challenge among the team. These are just some of the people issues and challenges we can face as we approach the collective work of student ministry.

Leaders who are students, parents who serve, volunteers who teach, or staff who oversee the challenges or issues become aspects that everyone on the team can sense or have to navigate. Each person should know the expectations and be equipped to navigate unfortunate challenges and issues. If something were to arise to the level of a physical threat, then it is important for the team to know the steps to take to handle the situation. Mental, emotional, and spiritual harm are challenges that require more training than a simple safety or security process for physical harm. Anytime you discern a potential issue of harm, then mandatory reporting is a step that has to be considered. If you determine not to report an issue with authorities, then you need to document your decision and why and who was consulted. Once you know the student is not a threat to themselves or others, then you need to help them seek counseling for an issue. I refer to Christian licensed counselors for issues that I cannot coach people through about their spiritual lives. Sometimes, family members are not open to helping their student, and you will need to discuss the next steps with your senior leader at your church or over your student ministry. If you are working through this resource with others, then discuss your plans for helping students. It may seem like a no-brainer, but prayer is key in this process as well.

Issues and challenges can arise with an individual student. A student can have a personal issue that is taken out on the youth group or church.

PAUSE & REFLECT

How should the student ministry prepare the team to navigate peer-to-peer issues within the student ministry?

Students need to develop redemptive interpersonal skills as they interact with each other. Usually, the action that is provoked is deep-seated from something that may not be obvious to the leader. A personal challenge that is left unchecked often leads to their destruction. As a leader, be the observing shepherd who is aware of signs of challenge with your people.

Issues and challenges can arise between students or families. People can have a conflict between the two parties. Recently, a parent shared with me about their middle school son being engaged in conflict with another middle school guy. They wanted to fight it out, so her son sent an Uber to pick up the guy. Since he could not drive, they could fight and handle their disagreement. This issue then becomes a problem for two families and is just one example of how the student ministry can be in the middle of students or families that have challenges with one another. When students begin to date, some parents are more open to the people their teenager chooses to date than others. When a dad does not like who his daughter is dating, then it can be tense among families in the church. We could continue to list possible scenarios for concerns with people, but the intended point is for you to be aware of the various angles from which people can create challenges or issues within the student ministry. You need plans and processes to have redemptive options for those who struggle and always be sure that the people within the ministry are safe. Does this issue involve only people within the student ministry or church, or is the issue a larger issue that involves people outside of your church? When an issue involves only people within the church, then we begin to teach students how to follow Matthew 18 in resolving conflict with another brother or sister in Christ. If the issue is outside the Church, but they are still a believer, then I teach students to follow Matthew 18 to seek reconciliation. If the issue is not with a believer, then we begin by discussing the spiritual nature that we have as Christians and how to deal with a conflict as we understand the need for another to see Christ in our actions.

LEADERSHIP CHALLENGES WITH PEOPLE

Issues and challenges can arise between a student and a team member of the student ministry. Challenges of authority can be delicate as a leader deals with a minor who is having an issue. The ability to have evidence of behavior when an issue or challenge arises is important to consider. Many people will not believe their child misbehaved or had an issue with leadership or others. Video surveillance can help people understand the nature of the issue. Everything will not be recorded, so you need to develop a consistent response within the ministry to deal with issues or challenges. People in our society do not appreciate perceived mistreatment, and so, as leaders, we have to have plans for issues so we are consistent in helping others.

Issues and challenges can arise between team members and senior leadership in the church. Leaders make decisions or take positions on issues that may cause people to question their leadership, but someone may not always have the full story because they are not the leader. A part of leading people is that people will eventually become disgruntled about something a leader says because we are people with our own opinions. A teacher in the student ministry may be upset with the pastor over an issue not related to the student ministry. A challenge within the church that spills into the student ministry can be delicate to navigate. One example would be a group of parents that begin to nudge people to think the student minister should replace the senior pastor. Just remember, if a person will talk to you about another leader, then they will eventually talk to someone else about you as a leader.

CHALLENGES WITH PROPERTY
Property can have many issues and challenges that have to be taken into consideration by the student ministry for special events and the weekly scheduled program. A safety concern during an event then becomes a people issue; a gas leak, power outage, or mechanical breakdown can cause a challenge, and students are not always well-equipped to handle unforeseen problems. Severe weather, bus breakdowns, or having to alter a plan can cause stress in the student ministry. Church leaders will need to develop their emergency action plans in advance and communicate those among their teams. I would begin by considering my people and their needs, then I would look at safe areas to gather inside the building if appropriate or nearby places to evacuate if needed, and then I would consider the programmed activity of the student ministry to determine these plans for on and off-site activities. I would travel with a medical bag, know where local providers for health care were located, and make sure I had an understanding of our surroundings to help be prepared in case something happened that was unexpected. If you have students with special needs, then these can cause them to respond in ways that can be harmful to others or themselves. These property challenges are also people issues because the safety of the people is always the priority as you interact with property. I am more worried about evacuating the building safely than saving the building.

These are not the only places issues or challenges can arise, but they give us a pathway of unpacking the topic and hopefully allow you and your team to consider how to handle issues and challenges and hopefully prevent future issues and challenges. In the past several decades, I have reflected that I thought I had observed or been in the middle of every aspect of issues and challenges in the church. As a seminary professor and former student minister, I get to consult a lot of churches and continue to be amazed each month at all the unique issues and challenges we face. I am going to highlight some of those without names or churches to provide you with a little touch of the emerging challenges and issues we are facing under the umbrella of student ministry. The following does not directly relate to a specific church that I have served but a church that their senior leadership reached out to for advice.

- I did not have students identifying as furies on my ministry bingo card. My life and ministry did not imagine a day when student ministry would have to clarify gender with more than two options.

- Students share personal pornographic images through apps and text and do not realize it is illegal to create, distribute, or possess such images.

- Mandatory reporting is neglected by senior leadership, who do not want to follow through and follow the law without trying to minimize the concern and simply report the issue to the proper authorities within 24 hours.

- I did not imagine a student ministry where more students were from broken homes than from nuclear homes.

- I did not fathom a world where you could live an avatar life on the web in an alternate realm digitally and fake the people around in your community as being someone else altogether at church.

As we close this chapter, I want you not to be discouraged because there are still so many things that are right with this generation and the Church. We see glimpses of revival as students come to faith in Christ, are discipled, and some are called to ministry and missions. However, to deal with the content of this chapter, we need to highlight some of the real challenges and issues as a pathway for redemptive solutions. Hopefully, this chapter will help the team come together and understand all the places the enemy is throwing darts at their work and how to navigate the minefield before us. Take time to pray over your ministry and concerns. Then, begin to make plans and processes for areas in which you are linking direction for a potential challenge or issue.

QUESTIONS TO CONSIDER

1. What positive actions are you taking to provide safety and security to the student ministry?

2. How could you improve the safety of your student ministry with people, property, and programmed activity?

3. Where are security challenges that you could address to enhance the security with programmed on and off-campus activities at your church?

CHAPTER 14
TRAINING AND EQUIPPING

Education for students has been a lifelong pursuit, as well as being trained and equipped with life skills to help them succeed. At their earliest age, they begin to grow to where they can walk, feed themselves, and develop greater autonomy. The ability to be a lifelong learner is part of the disciple's journey to learn, grow, and be equipped to serve.

I like to garden. As a kid, my family had a large garden, and we worked in it every year to plow, plant, and nurture fruits and vegetables. I learned a lot watching others, and my grandparents trained and equipped me so that today, I am able to plant a garden and follow the process of producing fruits and vegetables. I am training others as we do this as well since my kids are helping with gardening. Mom continues to provide insights about specific vegetables and how to cook or process them for the freezer. We enjoyed the outcome, but work was required to cultivate for a harvest. I have had to YouTube a few videos about certain items on how to grow in my climate or search for recipes for cooking. Although I was trained and equipped for gardening growing up, the ability and skills needed today require further training and experience for me to have a harvest today.

One aspect of training is the investment it requires from leadership and those serving to make themselves available to be poured into by others. You can see the model of investing in others throughout the New Testament. A few ideas from Jesus, Paul, and the disciples.

SPEND TIME TOGETHER
Invest in one another, as we see throughout the disciple's ministry in the New Testament. They continued to devote themselves to being taught

and fellowshipping together. The early church, throughout the book of Acts, shows us the dedication of people to equipping themselves to serve together. You can make training and equipping times for teaching and fellowship a regular part of the student ministry. A team that plays together stays together, which is a leadership lesson I was taught early on in my ministry. A team that prays together also stays focused on what matters. A good cookout for fellowship can also have a teaching time. You can discover many ways to eat and have conversations that, in the process, as we talk and share together, a natural process of equipping emerges. We can learn a lot from each other if we spend quality time together.

IRON SHARPENING IRON
Entrust to capable people. By being enlisted, a leader saw value in being entrusted to you and enlisted you to serve. An entrustment to serve by an organization is a great endorsement, but it should be a humbling experience to know someone saw something in you that caused them to pause and desire to train, and providing ongoing equipping is not an easy task. The time investment is great for providing ongoing coaching to someone. One of my favorite verses from Paul's writing to Timothy is when he encourages Timothy to invest in others. Paul says in 2 Timothy 2: 1-2, *"You then, my child, be strengthened by the grace that is in Christ Jesus, and what you have heard from me in the presence of many witnesses entrust to faithful men, who will be able to teach others also."* Paul encourages Timothy that what he has seen modeled and what he has learned from him to invest in others so that he will see and know how to live and model the Christian life as well. I love this visual reminder of how we live our lives and the impact it can have on others.

PAUSE & REFLECT

Ponder those who have impacted your life by sharpening you or causing you to strive to serve as a disciple. Make a list or write an encouraging note to someone who has helped to sharpen you. If possible, contact them to thank them for investing in your life. Conclude this reflection by spending time in prayer and thanking God for those in your life who have impacted you.

CALL OTHERS OUT TO SERVE
Develop the call to nurture the gifts and be equipped for the work of the church. Cultivate your ongoing ability to serve in student ministry.

The ongoing challenges that teenagers face and a shifting moral society cause challenges that are new for leaders. Some may think they are not able to answer the call to serve students. Each of us can call others out to serve. People need encouragement that you think they can serve. Do you remember a person who believed in you and nurtured you to serve? The cultivation of skills to communicate, teach, and mentor students is needed. Even the skill set of a high school student cultivating a relationship with a middle schooler requires training. The skills are the easier pieces to cultivate in student ministry. The hardest thing to remember is to encourage and celebrate with your people. We often have concerns or issues to solve and forget to provide a cultivating culture that has joy in the service. We have to train people to be encouraging. Students have enough challenges in their lives, so as a team, we need to be positive, encouraging people that point them to the only true source of hope.

Equipping others and growing in your own ability through serving can be challenging as we work together in ministry each week. "Entrust these things to capable people..." as Paul instructed, Timothy serves as a reminder to us that as disciples, we multiply through discipling other believers but also through utilizing our gifts as we serve in the church (2 Timothy 2:2). Teenagers are disciples that need to be discipled but also cultivated to serve. Adults and teenagers are representative of a key ministry of the church as students are developing their worldviews, lifestyles, and careers. Modeling the Christian life for other believers is the best way to develop others to be like Christ and serve His Church.

ONBOARDING TEAM MEMBERS
Placing people in positions of service can be a challenge. How does a person with their unique gifts make the biggest impact in the student ministry? We all consider, at some point, our difference-making impact. We look back over our lives and begin to consider whether we invested in the right people, whether we were involved in the right things, or whether we were committed to the most important aspects of Christ and His Church. Considering who each person is in Christ and how they fit within the composite of student ministry is an important step in onboarding people into the existing team of volunteers and staff.

One aspect that we each need to consider as we serve is what it is the model servant that we are trying to become, exhibit, or replicate. Many will be reminded of John's description in his gospel account of Jesus. Picture the setting with the towel and basin that was common to each household and how Jesus washed the disciples' feet. Have you ever washed someone's feet? A very humbling experience because you have to get down to your hands and feet and submit yourself in a posture of looking up to another person. This picture of service is one that is not modeled in society as a whole today but one that should not be lost on us within the church. We serve students, families, and the church as a picture of a towel and basin. You cannot do it with selfish motives when the focus of service is that of being a humble servant.

Training and equipping require each one of us to take time systematically over time to profile who we need to become, exhibit, or replicate. Sometimes, we need to be reminded of the risk factors with student ministry from events, facilities, or with students. Other weeks, we need to learn to communicate at a better level with students, families, and fellow team members. A disciple will keep striving to learn, grow, and become more like Christ. A formative thought for us to embrace is that we are in an ongoing cycle to submit to a process for training and equipping. Engaging in the process should not feel like the eye rolling of a corporate training video series that each employee has to complete or an all-called staff meeting for training that people walk to the conference room already bored; instead, people should be excited to be equipped to do better at the work of ministry with students. As you ponder the ways and areas that you offer training for student ministry, work to develop a process that sharpens the people. Develop ways to create chemistry among those serving so that they learn to spend time together and enjoy the company of one another. Jesus told us the harvest is plentiful, but the workers are few. The work to equip those that we have and cultivate people to serve will be an ongoing endeavor and may even be discouraging at times. Investing in a workforce that links arms and creates a healthy student ministry makes an amazing impact for generations.

QUESTIONS TO CONSIDER

1. Take a moment to describe the characteristics of a model servant. I encourage you to read the following: Joshua 24:15, John 13, 1 Corinthians 12. As you read each passage, then make notes of what is being described as you serve.

2. Joshua 24:15 Joshua had already reminded the people to serve Like Moses with all their heart and soul in Joshua 22:5, and now, a few verses later, he asks if serving the Lord is disagreeable to you. As you read these verses, ponder how serving the Lord week in and week out could be disagreeable to you.

3. John 13:5-20 describes Jesus washing the disciple's feet. How does the picture of Jesus washing feet and describing the action as an example for them to follow impact your picture of how you serve in student ministry?

4. Paul takes an exhaustive explanation of gifts and how the body fits together as each person is utilizing their gifts (1 Corinthians 12). Paul says we thrive or suffer as we serve using our gifts. In the student ministry, do you see each member helping the overall team thrive or suffer? How so?

CHAPTER 15
CLARIFYING QUESTIONS

We conclude our discussion on serving in student ministry with five clarifying questions that each member should answer. You may add to this list for your assessment of how the student ministry is working as you serve together. These five questions focus on the students, their families, the volunteers, the student ministry, and the local church.

QUESTION 1: WHAT DOES THE STUDENT NEED?
Hopefully, you are not frustrated by this question, but this question is a reminder that in the local church, the student ministry is trying to solve the spiritual formation needs of students and continue to be the front line for sharing the Gospel with students. This is the type of question that should help to refocus those serving in the ministry but also challenge each team member to consider the needs of students. We can easily become focused on repeating the previous events or assume that the needs of your students will be the same next year. I encourage you to spend time as a team and as individuals to consider the primary needs of your students. You may discover in this process that new challenges or issues have surfaced that need to be grafted into your student ministry plan with students.

QUESTION 2: WHAT DO THE PARENTS/GUARDIANS NEED?
The parents, who are the primary influencers on student's lives, are not always considered in the overall ministry plan for student ministry. As you consider the macro picture of the student ministry team, how do the parents find the strategy as part of the overall team? When considering the team members, most parents did not experience today's realities. They did not have transgender students trying to play female sports as biological males. They did not have a smartphone or online gaming as constant

connectivity options. They had technology, they had gaming consoles, and they had cultural experiences, but all of those seem archaic to the current generation of students. It is interesting to consider that each generation of students looks at their parent's experiences with life as archaic. The basic needs of teenagers have not changed if you consider their physical well-being, spiritual development, emotional stability, and mental wholeness. Parents desire to be connected to the lives of their teenagers if they are connected to the church. You see some student ministries offering parent-equipping workshops on youth discipleship or youth culture. In addition to parenting options, churches continue to consider ways to connect parents through family ministry options, whether a retreat or an ongoing Bible study series. The student families need to be able to grow together in their relationship with Christ. Students may not have parents overseeing their spiritual development, and thus, grandparents or other adult mentors serve as spiritual guardians for those students at church. Many students have parents in their lives, but more come from broken homes or absentee parents. The Church needs to recognize that those spiritual guardians may need to be included in the equipping of adults in the student ministry.

QUESTION 3: WHAT DOES THE STUDENT MINISTRY NEED?

This may seem like an unusual question, but the ministry itself has needs based on the strategy being employed. We could spend an entire book discussing various strategies for approaching student ministry, but we will keep this question to the major needs that are common among student ministries. Each person serving has to consider the larger perspective of student ministry as a point of reference for what is needed and not your personal opinion. The student ministry has a vision of desired outcomes, and each team member that is serving needs to understand their vital piece of achieving those objectives. The current iteration of student ministry in your church is vital to the spiritual health of students, to develop their worldview, and to create a faith that lasts.

QUESTION 4: WHAT DOES THE MINISTRY VOLUNTEER NEED?

This is not a sarcastic insight into our work, but oftentimes, the organization (the church or student ministry) thinks about what they need within and not what the individual needs to be asked to join the team in any capacity. Burnout has become a common word in ministry circles, and the overall health of those serving is something that no leader can tackle alone. Everyone needs to help each other and look for signs of fatigue, spiritual stagnation, or a loss of love for the area in student ministry they are filling. Each person is supposed to utilize their gifts and talents within the church, but is that to the level of depletion or ongoing replenishment? If you pick a verse here or there, you can find support that might indicate both could be true. The bigger issue is that the volunteer is simply a volunteer. They have more in their life than this one aspect, and we have to develop safeguards to help the team navigate the ongoing struggle of serving beyond capacity or reaching the point of a negative return. A team member also needs to be discipled as part of the process of serving. We grow as followers better through our service, but that impact can extend when an intentional pathway exists for those servings to help them grow.

QUESTION 5: WHAT DOES THE CHURCH NEED?
You may be thinking the obvious answer is volunteers serving in student ministry since the book is focused on serving in student ministry. Yes, the big goal is to have a workforce of paid and volunteer staff that reach and make disciples with teenagers and their families. A people that lives out Micah 6:8 through acting justly, loving faithfulness, and walking humbly with the Lord. Sometimes, the church desires a strong student ministry, but they do not realize the long-term impact on the church as each generation is the church of today but with a future adult leadership workforce that will lead and thrive in the church or depart the church altogether, leaving their adolescent faith behind. The church needs a strong student ministry for today so that the next generation of the church can be reached.

Each of these questions has a basic answer, but they will also be nuanced based on regional factors, family dynamics, church settings, and the overall influence of student ministry in the community. The critical questions cover five areas that need to be revisited at least annually to be sure any changes have not caused the student ministry to drift in one or more of the areas. If you have ever been on a boat in a larger body of water or hiking in the woods, you realize how easy it is to drift, of course, by little increments that greatly impact the destination. I have been driving the boat, looking back, and realized that when I could not see the land in any direction, it would be easy to get off course. One day, working in the woods getting ready for the hunting season, I thought getting back after scouting would be easy until everything looked the same in each direction. I am thankful that in both situations, I had a compass to help focus the direction I was headed and was able to arrive exactly where I needed to be. Serving in ministry is much the same way. As we get into the work and put our life behind it, then we are working and striving, but if we don't intentionally take moments to check our coordinates, each of us can drift, of course. Even as a ministry team, we can drift off the intended mark.

PAUSE & REFLECT

Take some time to reflect on your responsibilities in student ministry and consider your contribution to responding to the needs represented in your church. As you do this, follow that with a time of prayer for your students, their families, the student ministry, the church, and your needs. If you can schedule a time to be alone and reflect for a few hours, a personal retreat can be helpful as you pray, journal, and consider the impact of student ministry on so many people. The work that we do in student ministry impacts eternity, and you are a vital part of the student ministry workforce. You are a part of not just your church but countless thousands of people who are giving their lives to serve students.

Each of us fits within a large context of people serving the Lord. We will have a filter through our lens of experience, culture, spiritual growth, and family that influences how we may approach serving in student ministry. I implore you to work to be a person who understands the needs of the people serving you and the students and families you are ministering to at your church. Cultivating a team to serve requires each of us to work together to understand the needs and how we each think and approach our roles on the team. As we begin to understand these questions and factors, we become healthy team members and effectively impact those around us. I am praying for you as I lift up all those serving in student ministry to accomplish this task well.

QUESTIONS TO CONSIDER

1. You were prompted to ask yourself five questions as you read the chapter. Of those five, what is the biggest need in your student ministry that is an ongoing hurdle for you?

2. How can you improve your process of considering what needs exist within your student ministry?

3. Where do you feel you are doing well in meeting the needs of your student ministry? What are you doing in order to meet these needs?

CONCLUSION

I believe a disciple serving in ministry is one of the greatest privileges we have as Christians. Students benefit greatly when we choose to work together as a team, whether we are paid or volunteer. People do not arrive at their current destination without people investing in their lives, both positive and negative. People will also be a part of the future story that is written. In God's plan, He created the Church so that we could worship and thrive, utilizing our gifts to encourage one another. These chapters were crafted to help student ministry leaders begin discussions and conversations about how team members could grow in the primary areas people may encounter as they serve. The list was not exhaustive, but hopefully, it will help you think about your own growth and leadership with others. My prayer for you as you serve in student ministry is that you will keep striving to grow and listen to the Lord and others in your life to understand the needs of the generation you are working to reach and disciple.

We started with the reminder to serve selflessly, as modeled by Jesus. Each generation has been influenced by different factors and can contribute to learning from each other in ministry. We continued with a challenge to being faithful to the work that we have been called to serve. This challenge to being faithful leads us to fulfill our needed component within the local church. Each of us must stay engaged in our devotion to the Lord. Students need us to provide care for them through our service. The motivation of being self-directed in our willingness to grow, learn, and lead in student ministry should be evident as we serve. Servant leaders should become more like Christ by serving in the student ministry.

In addition, student ministry leaders must be faithful to church involvement. As we live for Christ, we also observe the influences that culture has on us as well as students and how those factors impact each person's worldview. Each generation has been impacted through different life events, family experiences, and education, which can impact how the generations interact with one another. We find that each generation is needed in the Church, which means we have to look for the interests of each group as well as the individuals within the student ministry.

We looked at how to better understand people by communicating with one another. We understand that the world is not as safe and secure as previous generations may have observed, so we need to understand the challenges of today and not just the past. Since all these factors and more impact us, each team needs to commit to ongoing training to be equipped for the ongoing work of student ministry. We conclude with a few questions to help you consider the various needs that should be prayed over and considered in your student ministry.

The study guide that follows provides a resource for team development. The study guide, which was written by a student minister who serves each week with students, should be read through and discussed together. The heart behind the words comes from experience but also the current reality of ministering to students today. May you be strengthened through the investment of working through this book and study guide.

STUDY GUIDE

CHAPTER 1

MAIN SCRIPTURE:

> And he gave the apostles, the prophets, the evangelists, the shepherds and teachers, to equip the saints for the work of ministry, for building up the body of Christ.
> — *Ephesians 4:11-12*

BOTTOM LINE:
In student ministry, the call to serve selflessly is rooted in the model given to us by Jesus. Serving selflessly gives us the opportunity to make Jesus known to students.

QUESTIONS FOR ADULT SERVE TEAM:
1. How has serving in our church helped you grow in your faith and leadership?

2. What do you love the most about serving? Why?

3. Are there people not with us today that could be serving with us? Who?

4. What's been your most challenging moment in serving?

5. If you were trying to tell someone to serve in the church, what would you say to them?

CHAPTER 2

MAIN SCRIPTURE:

One generation shall commend your works to another and shall declare your mighty acts.
— Psalm 145:4

BOTTOM LINE:
Student ministry can leverage generational influences to remind adults that the future is bright as students desire to grow in Christ and be a part of the Church.

QUESTIONS FOR ADULT SERVE TEAM:
1. How do students benefit from having an intergenerational ministry?

2. What impact has a younger generation had in your life?

3. What impact has an older generation had in your life?

4. What are other ideas we can incorporate in an intergenerational ministry approach?

5. Which generation most represents our adult leaders? Do we need to work to have other generations around us to help create a broader intergenerational ministry approach?

CHAPTER 3

MAIN SCRIPTURE:

> For just as the body is one and has many members, and all the members of the body, though many, are one body, so it is with Christ.
> — 1 Corinthians 12:12

BOTTOM LINE:
The simple task of fulfilling the mission of being a part of a team is to be found faithful in your work and committed to the overall health of the ministry.

QUESTIONS FOR ADULT SERVE TEAM:
1. What is your definition of a healthy team?

2. What can you do to help our team feel more unified and work towards the same goal?

3. What would it look like to celebrate one another on our team? What things could we celebrate?

4. Do you feel like you have everything you need to be successful on the team? What are you missing? What do you need more of? What works best?

5. What's the hardest part of being on a team? How do you combat that?

CHAPTER 4

MAIN SCRIPTURE:

> You then, my child, be strengthened by the grace that is in Christ Jesus, and what you have heard from me in the presence of many witnesses entrust to faithful men, who will be able to teach others also.
> — 2 Timothy 2:1-2

BOTTOM LINE:
As Christians, each of us is called to ministry and has a purpose of service in the church.

QUESTIONS FOR ADULT SERVE TEAM:

1. How would you define a mentor in the context of student ministry?

2. What qualities or characteristics are essential for someone based on the different age groups they are mentoring?

3. Who is someone who mentored you? What stands out about him/her?

4. What's different about serving a group of middle schoolers or high schoolers? Do you feel like you connect better with one or the other?

5. What are practical steps you can take to help recruit and retain other volunteers?

CHAPTER 5

MAIN SCRIPTURE:

> And they devoted themselves to the apostles' teaching and the fellowship.
>
> — Acts 2:42

BOTTOM LINE:
The most extraordinary growth for Christians comes through their personal devotion to the Lord and linking arms out of their dedication to serve others and the church.

QUESTIONS FOR ADULT SERVE TEAM:

1. Take some time together and explore the diversity of giftedness among the team. What did you learn about one another?

2. How do you see God using your spiritual gifts? What other gifts or talents do you have that God can use?

3. How is the church different from other tribes in our lives? How can we help our students see that?

4. Read Acts 2:42-47. What stands out to you about the devotion of the early church? Why? What areas can our youth group grow to be more like the early church?

5. Are there certain parts of serving in youth ministry that are difficult? Why? How can you encourage others to stay devoted to the task?

CHAPTER 6

MAIN SCRIPTURE:

> Commit your work to the Lord, and your plans will be established.
> — Proverbs 16:3

BOTTOM LINE:
Demonstrating as a leader that you are committed, available, relatable, and an example is needed to develop a strong connection to care for students in the student ministry.

QUESTIONS FOR ADULT SERVE TEAM:
1. Out of the C.A.R.E. acronym, which quality do you struggle with the most? Why?

2. How does commitment to serving in youth ministry compare to other commitments in your life?

3. How can a volunteer's availability impact students and our team?

4. How do you balance the tension of being relatable to students while not trying to look "cool?"

5. How do you live out C.A.R.E. to students outside of church?

CHAPTER 7

MAIN SCRIPTURE:

I can do all things through him who strengthens me.
— Philippians 4:13

BOTTOM LINE:
A servant leader is one who sees something needs to be done and is one who does not wait for instructions for simple needs.

QUESTIONS FOR ADULT SERVE TEAM:

1. What motivates you to serve in student ministry? How does this motivation impact your responsibilities as a leader?

2. What challenges do you face in being self-directed/motivated? How do you overcome those?

3. Think of a time when you saw someone else on our team take initiative without being asked. How did that inspire you?

4. What specific ways can we help middle schoolers to be more self-directed/motivated?

5. What specific ways can we help high schoolers to be more self-directed/motivated?

CHAPTER 8

MAIN SCRIPTURE:

And Jesus called them to him and said to them, "You know that those who are considered rulers of the Gentiles lord it over them, and their great ones exercise authority over them. But it shall not be so among you. But whoever would be great among you must be your servant, and whoever would be first among you must be slave of all. For even the Son of Man came not to be served but to serve, and to give his life as a ransom for many."

— Mark 10:42-45

BOTTOM LINE:
The servant leader is focused more on becoming more like Christ in the pursuit of pleasing God and becoming holy.

QUESTIONS FOR ADULT SERVE TEAM:

1. How are you growing in your relationship with Christ? What is something you have learned in your own personal time with the Lord?

2. What are some practical ways we can help middle school students model servanthood?

3. What are some practical ways we can help high school students model servanthood?

4. How do we help others in the church who aren't serving see the need for serving and the reward it brings?

5. What are ways we can help each other prioritize growing in our faith?

CHAPTER 9

MAIN SCRIPTURE:

> And let us consider how to stir up one another to love and good works, not neglecting to meet together, as is the habit of some, but encouraging one another, and all the more as you see the day is near.
> — Hebrews 10:24-25

BOTTOM LINE:

The need to engage with other believers and the church and not just show up to deplete a person's resource through serving is crucial in maintaining a healthy team of people invested in student ministry.

QUESTIONS FOR ADULT SERVE TEAM:

1. Why is it important to be engaged in the whole church (serving and being in worship)?

2. What are things this group can do to help make sure nobody here gets burnt out from serving?

3. What are ways we can encourage and provide opportunities for students to serve in the church?

4. What do you think our church considers "engaged?" Why?

5. When did you realize the importance of being an engaged member of our church?

CHAPTER 10

MAIN SCRIPTURE:

> Great is the Lord, and greatly to be praised, and his greatness is unsearchable. One generation shall commend your works to another, and shall declare your mighty acts.
> — Psalm 145:3-4

BOTTOM LINE:
Student ministry is an evolving process of understanding each generation.

QUESTIONS FOR ADULT SERVE TEAM:

1. What are things you love about youth culture right now?

2. What are things that drive you crazy about youth culture?

3. Does our youth ministry do a good job of meeting students where they are today? What can we do better or different?

4. Does our youth group have its own culture? If so, how would you describe it?

5. What are things we can do to stay current on youth culture trends? Why does that matter?

CHAPTER 11

MAIN SCRIPTURE:

> *Above all, keep loving one another earnestly, since love covers a multitude of sins. Show hospitality to one another without grumbling. As each has received a gift, use it to serve one another, as good stewards of God's varied grace.*
> — 1 Peter 4:8-10

BOTTOM LINE:
A person who is focused on ministry is willing to look out for the interest of others and not just their needs.

QUESTIONS FOR ADULT SERVE TEAM:
1. What types of teams have you served on in the past? What did you enjoy about them? What do you enjoy about this one?

2. From the acronym T.E.A.M., which area do you want to see yourself grow in? Why?

3. How do you balance being available to students? What are ways you've made yourself available?

4. In what ways are you growing as a leader in our ministry? What resources have you found to help you?

5. How can we help new volunteers plug into our team and feel welcome?

CHAPTER 12

MAIN SCRIPTURE:

> Let your speech always be gracious, seasoned with salt, so that you may know how you ought to answer each person.
> — Colossians 4:6

BOTTOM LINE:
Good communication is a vital factor in a healthy student ministry.

QUESTIONS FOR ADULT SERVE TEAM:
1. What is it like communicating with students? Do you find it funny, frustrating, or surprising?

2. Do you communicate with the parents of your students? If not, why? What are effective ways we can communicate to parents?

3. Do you feel like you are communicated well to as a leader from the church staff? What would you add or take away?

4. How do you filter what is appropriate to say to a student?

5. Do you feel like we have a strong sense of communication within our volunteer team? Are there other ways we can communicate with each other that would be helpful?

CHAPTER 13

MAIN SCRIPTURE:

> Be angry and do not sin; do not let the sun go down on your anger, and give no opportunity to the devil.
> — Ephesians 4:26-27

BOTTOM LINE:
As a leader, be the observing shepherd who is aware of signs of challenge with your people.

QUESTIONS FOR ADULT SERVE TEAM:

1. How have you handled issues, challenges, and conflicts with your students?

2. How do we help our students see a biblical model of how to approach relational issues?

3. How do we, as a volunteer team, work towards maintaining unity?

4. What are some of the biggest challenges you have faced in student ministry? How did you respond to this?

5. What are some potential challenges we might face in our student ministry? Are there steps or conversations we can begin to have now that can help prepare us or even prevent them from happening?

CHAPTER 14

MAIN SCRIPTURE:

> *Have nothing to do with irreverent, silly myths. Rather train yourself for godliness; for while bodily training is of some value, godliness is of value in every way, as it holds promise for the present life and also for the life to come.*
> — 1 Timothy 4:7-8

BOTTOM LINE:
We serve students, families, and the church as a picture of a towel and basin. You cannot do it with selfish motives when the focus of service is that of being a humble servant.

QUESTIONS FOR ADULT SERVE TEAM:
1. Do you find value in being trained and equipped as a leader? Why?

2. What are areas you would like training and equipping on?

3. Do you feel like we have a good onboarding experience for new volunteers? Why or why not? What changes can we make in this area to make it better?

4. What are things you've learned from leading in our ministry that you could share with others to help them grow?

5. Who are some people in our church we could call out to serve in our ministry?

CHAPTER 15

MAIN SCRIPTURE:

> Let no one despise you for your youth, but set believers an example in speech, in conduct, in love, in faith, in purity.
> — 1 Timothy 4:12

BOTTOM LINE:
As a leader, be aware of the needs of students, families, and the church.

QUESTIONS FOR ADULT SERVE TEAM:
1. What would you say students need the most from our ministry? Why?

2. What would you say parents need the most from our ministry? Why?

3. What things do we need to incorporate in our ministry? Why?

4. Does our student ministry feel like it is part of the greater church, or does it feel like a separate "thing" of the church? Why?

5. What do you need as a volunteer to stay healthy, serve for years, and grow in your faith?

ABOUT THE AUTHOR

Jody Dean serves as Professor of Christian Education, Director of the Doctor of Education Programs, and Director of the Church Training Institute at New Orleans Baptist Theological Seminary. For most of his adult life, Jody has been devoted to serving the local church and equipping people to make disciples. Over the past decade, he has been specifically focused on developing another generation of leaders to equip people and love the local church. As a professor, Jody focuses his research and teaching on the topics of discipleship, church administration, risk management, age-group ministry, and leadership development. These five areas are favorites for him to teach, research, write about, and speak on. Outside of the classroom, Jody has continued to serve the local church for over twenty years in the areas of discipleship and administration. He has numerous years of ministry experience serving inside the local church and leading in children's ministry, youth ministry, collegiate ministry, adult ministry, and as an interim Senior Associate Pastor. When he's not in the classroom or serving within the church, you will find Jody teaching at conferences and training events in churches, regional training events, state conventions, and organizations for ministers in the local church. Jody is married to Emily, and they have two children, Lydia and James Robert.

AS A YOUTH MINISTER, YOU WANT TO LEAD STUDENTS TO BE MORE LIKE CHRIST.

THE QUESTION IS, HOW DO YOU GO ABOUT DOING IT?

DISCIPLE: The Ordinary Person's Guide to Discipling Teenagers is a practical, down-to-earth guide for leading teenagers to pursue Christ.

GET SERIOUS ABOUT DISCIPLE-MAKING IN YOUR MINISTRY WITH *DISCIPLE*.

FOR SAMPLES & ORDERING INFO, GO TO YM360.COM/DISCIPLE.

ANOTHER GREAT RESOURCE FROM JODY DEAN

ORDER TODAY AT YM360.COM/PROTECT AND YOU'LL BE EQUIPPED TO NAVIGATE THE CHALLENGES AND RISKS IN YOUTH MINISTRY TODAY!

GENERATE
CAMP BY YM360

5 DAYS OF CAMP THAT CAN CHANGE THE OTHER 51 WEEKS OF YOUR YEAR, YOUR LIFE, AND MAYBE EVEN YOUR GENERATION.

GENERATESTUDENTS.COM